The Regulations of Purity and Impurity in Islam

Proceedings of the 8th AMI Contemporary Fiqhī Issues Workshop, 2–3 July 2020

Proceedings of the AMI Contemporary Fiqhī Issues Workshop

VOLUME 2

The Regulations of Purity and Impurity in Islam

Proceedings of the
8th AMI Contemporary Fiqhī Issues Workshop
2–3 July, 2020

Edited by
Hashim Bata

AMI PRESS

THE REGULATIONS OF PURITY AND IMPURITY IN ISLAM

PROCEEDINGS OF THE 8th AMI CONTEMPORARY FIQHĪ ISSUES WORKSHOP, 2–3 JULY 2020

ISBN 978-1-915550-00-2

Design and typesetting by Wahid M. Amin

Printed in the United Kingdom

CONTENTS

List of Contributors vii

Introduction: The Regulations of Purity and Impurity in Islam 1

Hashim Bata

The Role of Purity and Impurity Regulations in the Formation of the Muslim Economy in the Early Period of Islam 8

Reza Pourmohammadi

The Structure and Message of al-Kulaynī's Book of Purity: A Modern Reading of a Classical Text 23

Stephen Burge

Online Narratives on Menstruation, Public Conversations, and Relationships with Religious Law 54

Krista M. Riley

Religious Purity and Impurity from Different Perspectives 67

Ali Fanaei

The Existential Perspective on the Meaning and Implication of Impure Substances within Shīʿī Jurisprudential Discourse 79

Arif Abdul Hussain

Hashim Bata

is a lecturer and one of the directors at the Al-Mahdi Institute. He is also an associate lecturer in Islamic studies at the University of Birmingham. He completed seminary (Ḥawza) studies at the Al-Mahdi Institute and attained a PhD from the Department of Law at the University of Warwick in 2014, which focused on the legal epistemology of Modern Shīʿī *uṣūl al-fiqh*. Dr Bata contributed a chapter in *Visions of Sharia: Contemporary Discussions in Shīʿī Legal Theory* and is currently in the process of publishing his monograph *Exploring the Mind of God: An Introduction to Shiite Legal Theory.*

Stephen Burge

is Senior Research Associate at The Institute of Ismaili Studies. He completed his PhD at the University of Edinburgh. In addition to several published articles, he is the author of two monographs, *Angels in Islam: Jalāl al-Dīn al-Suyūṭī's al-Ḥabā'ik fī akhbār al-malā'ik* and *The Prophet Muhammad: Islam and the Divine Message*. He has also edited *The Meaning of the Word: Lexicology and Qur'anic Exegesis*. He also co-edited *The Making of Religious Texts in Islam: The Fragment and the Whole*. He is currently co-editing and translating a volume on the *Anthology of Quranic Commentaries Series on the Pillars of Islam*. His main research interests are the works of Jalāl al-Dīn al-Suyūṭī, *ḥadīth* studies, *tafsīr* (Qur'anic exegesis) and angelology. He is also an Anglican Priest.

Ali Fanaei

received his PhD in Philosophy from the University of Sheffield after having completed 17 years of seminary studies at the Hawza Ilmiyya of Qum where he attended advanced sessions taught by leading experts such as Ayatollah Mohaghegh Damad, Ayatollah Tabrizi, Ayatollah Ha'iri, Ayatollah Wahid Khorasani, Ayatollah Montazeri, and Ayatollah Ahmad Mianeji. Alongside his teaching activities at the Al-Mahdi Institute and Mofid University of Qum, he is the author of numerous publications in English and Farsi. Dr. Fanaei is currently regarded as one of the leading figures of the *rowshan fikrī* ('enlightenment thinkers') school and has made several appearances on broadcast media in Iran.

Arif Abdul Hussain

is the director and founder of the Al-Mahdi Institute, where he lectures in *uṣūl al-fiqh* and philosophy. He has been at the forefront of developing and delivering advanced Islamic studies in the UK and has been lecturing on Islam for over twenty years, having in the process attained an international reputation as one of the most critical thinkers in the contemporary Muslim world. He is also the author of the *Islam and God-centricity* series, a collection of works exploring the author's own existential philosophy and its application across a wide variety of theological and legal issues in Islam.

Reza Pourmohammadi

is a faculty member at the Women's Research Centre in Iran. He completed his PhD in Islamic Law on the Status of Common Sense in Islamic Jurisprudence at the seminary of Qum. Currently he is finishing a second PhD in private law at the University of Shahid Beheshti in Tehran. Dr Pourmohammadi's research interests lie in the field of Islamic law and *uṣūl al-fiqh*. He has published several books and articles on Islamic law.

Krista Melanie Riley

holds a PhD in Communication Studies from Concordia University, where her research focused on practices of religious interpretation among Muslim feminist bloggers in North America. She works as a pedagogical counsellor and researcher at Vanier College in Montreal. Her current research project looks at the experiences of Muslim college students in Quebec.

HASHIM BATA

Introduction: The Regulations of Purity and Impurity in Islam

This volume presents a collection of papers from the 8th Contemporary Fiqhī Issues Workshop held at Al-Mahdi Institute (AMI) in July 2020. The topic of the workshop concerned Sharia regulations of purity (*ṭahāra*) and impurity (*najāsa*) and their practical, socio-ethical, and theological implications. This topic is of immense relevance to present-day Muslims, as juristic (or the *fiqhī*) interpretation of Sharia regulations of purity and impurity not only affect the personal daily hygiene and spirituality of individual Muslims, but also informs their wider socio-communal and economic relations and interactions. These regulations broadly form the bases for Islamic dietary requirements; commerce and trading etiquettes; genital, toiletry, and sexual hygiene; and stipulate how a Muslim ought to purify themselves prior to performing ritual acts of worship such as the daily prayers (*ṣalāt*), fasting in the month of Ramadan (*ṣawm*), pilgrimage to Mecca (Hajj), etc. Most orthodox Muslim jurists (*fuqahā'*) categorise substances such as blood, urine, faeces, semen, dead bodies, dogs, pigs, and alcoholic beverages as being essentially impure (*al-najis al-ʿayn*). Additionally, most Shīʿī jurists also categorise non-Muslims or unbelievers (*kuffār*) as being essentially impure. Muslim jurists uphold that if an essentially impure substance is to touch, particularly if it is wet, an object (whether the object is a human being or a utensil), then the object becomes impure (or *mutanajjis*), and it is obligatory upon a Muslim to purify it with purifying agents (*muṭahhirāt*) such as water, sunlight, earth, or even conversion to Islam, etc.

To obtain a profound understanding of the juristic interpretation of Sharia regulations concerning purity and impurity and their implications on everyday Muslims, the workshop sought a multi-disciplinary approach. It brought together and facilitated leading seminary-trained Muslim jurists and theologians together with academics from a verity of fields and specialisms to share and discuss their research on Islamic purity laws and the cultures around them. Scholars and participants presented papers and posed questions that led to rich analytical discissions surrounding the topic. Some of the more thought-provoking interchanges that surfaced at the workshop included discussions concerning the historical, socio-political, and economic contexts in which

Sharia regulations of purity and impurity originated, and the impact of these contextual factors on their subsequent codification within the juristic discourse of different Muslim schools of jurisprudence; the theological foundations and epistemological assumptions that influence the hermeneutical methodology employed by Muslim jurists in their deduction of these regulations; empirical deliberations surrounding the present-day reception of these regulations and their ramifications on the social and personal lives of Muslims. It is important to note that the contributions made at the workshop highlighted that the prevalent juristic – or *fiqhī* – deduction of specific Sharia regulations of purity and impurity that pose major challenges to present-day Muslims include:

- *Fiqhī* regulations related to the impurity of female menstruation and their implication for female participation in ritual acts of worship such as daily prayers, fasting, pilgrimage, or even going inside certain mosques and shrines.

- *Fiqhī* regulations related to trading with, or being in the presence of, impure substances such as alcohol or pig/pork. Since such substances form an ostensible part of modern western societies in which they are regularly consumed and traded in public places, regulations related to their impurity at times pose problems for Muslims who reside or work in western countries.

- *Fiqhī* regulations related to the impurity of non-Muslims or unbelievers. These regulations pose a range of challenges for Muslims who reside or work within majority non-Muslim countries, ranging from broad socio-communal interactions and marital relations between Muslims and non-Muslims to specific dietary matters, such as the impermissibility of consuming meat slaughtered (or even general food prepared) by non-Muslims.

The first contribution to this volume is by Reza Pourmohammadi, whose study focuses on the historical context of the formative period of Islam when Sharia regulations of purity and non-purity originated. Pourmohammadi describes the socio-economic strength of the polytheists in the Arabian Peninsula and assesses the impact of their trading boycotts on the early Muslim community. He asserts that the polytheist boycotts and policies against the early Muslim community led it to encounter severe financial difficulties and poverty. His analysis carefully impresses that the contextual backdrop of a dire economic situation experienced by early Muslims was perhaps a significant factor that gave rise to the inauguration of Sharia regulations concerning purity and impurity. As such, he alludes that one of the purposes (or outcomes) of such regulations was that they allowed early Muslims to create a dynamic and strong domestic economic system that primarily profited the Muslim community settled in Medina. By highlighting Sharia regulations related to the impurity (and thereby the prohibition) of beverages and foods such as alcohol, pork, and animals slaughtered by non-Muslims, Pourmohammadi draws out the interrelation between Sharia, economy, and marketplace. His survey elucidates that in the present-day, Sharia (or more accurately, *fiqhī*) categorisations of pure and impure substances continues to impact and influence Muslim domestic economic systems.

After presenting an analysis of the historical context in which Sharia regulations of purity and impurity originated, the second contribution to this volume is by Stephen Burge, who explores their compilation within the corpus of *ḥadīth* literature. Burge studies the compilation of reports (*akhbār*) of the Prophet and Shīʿī Imāms related to purity and impurity in *Kitāb al-ṭahāra* (Book of Purity) that is found in the famous *ḥadīth* collection entitled *al-Kāfī fī ʿilm al-dīn* of the renowned tenth-century Shīʿī *ḥadīth* complier (*muḥaddith*) Muḥammad b. Yaʿqūb al-Kulaynī (d. 329/941). Following from Andrew Newman's conclusions in *The Formative Period of Twelver Shīʿism* (2013), Burge uses Kulaynī's compilation of *Kitāb al-ṭahāra* to exemplify that the method by which *ḥadīth* compliers arrange their collection of reports reveals their thought process and the ideologies they subscribe to and wish to emphasise and promulgate. Although Burge admits that Kulaynī's compilation of *Kitāb al-ṭahāra* is not a work of juristic deductions (or *fiqh*), he asserts that reports within it are arranged in a systematic, coherent, and ordered fashion that convey his Shīʿī ideological leanings and biases. Burge explains that Kulaynī's method of compilation subtly engages in dialogue with, or a polemic against, mainstream Sunni juristic deductions of Sharia regulations related to the rituals of purity. It thereby armours the Shīʿī community with sufficient evidence to justify and defend their own methods of performing rituals of purity within a broader Sunni context. Moreover, Burge points out that in contrast to Sunni *ḥadīth* compliers, Kulaynī's method of compilation overtly lays emphasis on deeper spiritual aspects of Sharia rituals of purity and as such is supportive of the overall esoteric ethos of Shīʿism.

Diverging from theoretical and historical discussions, Krista Riley's contribution in this volume assesses the practical impact that Sharia regulations of purity and impurity have on the lives of present-day Muslims. Riley explores the narratives of three Muslim feminist bloggers who have written on the evocative topic of mensuration. It is important to know that the Arabic term used to describe menstruation is *ḥayḍ*. According to Muslim jurists, menses are impure and therefore whilst a Muslim woman is menstruating she is prohibited from having sexual intercourse or performing ritual acts of worship that are otherwise obligatory, such as daily prayers, fasting in the month of Ramadan, circumambulating the Kaʿba during pilgrimage, etc. After a Muslim woman completes her menses, she is required to purify herself by performing ritual lustration known as *ghusl* – only then can she resume partaking in ritual acts of worship. Riley explores responses that female Muslim bloggers provide to the personal challenges and expectations they face from the socio-cultural and dominant juristic understanding of Sharia regulations related to mensuration. Riley explains that her reason for exploring feminist blogs is because they disclose immediate insights into the lived experiences of Muslim women, as digital media offers them with a platform where they can openly discuss and share their thoughts on a topic that is often considered as private both within and outside the Muslim context. Riley's study finds that, through blogging, Muslim females are providing alternate avenues and explanations of how the topic of, or topics related to, mensuration can be understood; specifically, those related topics that are normally absent within the orthodox Muslim juristic discourse. Riley propounds that by participating in blogs, Muslim women not only get to share their experiences and their religious perspectives, but that this platform also impacts and informs other Muslim women who go through similar experiences. In essence, Riley's study innovatively attempts to establish how new mediums of communication like blogging (or 'public conversations') intervene, reconfigure, and influence religious laws and debates about gender and sexuality.

The final two contributions in this volume are by Ali Fanaei and Arif Abdul Hussain. As alumni of traditional seminaries, both contributors offer insider-perspectives on how Sharia regulations of purity and impurity can be understood using alterative hermeneutical approaches that counter ones proffered by orthodox jurists. Fanaei's contribution highlights that the religious/juristic discourse of purity and impurity has become an integral part of Muslim identity. By focusing on the Shīʿī juristic notion of the physical impurity of non-Muslims, Fanaei opines that although such deductions of Sharia regulations have historically determined the way in which Muslims construct and maintain political, legal, and social relationships with non-Muslims, in today's era they can be criticised for being incompatible with basic civil and human rights and for deterring peaceful coexistence between Muslims and non-Muslims. Fanaei elucidates that the rich, extensive, and systematic juristic discourse on Sharia purity and impurity is merely focused on physical or bodily aspects of pollutants, whereas discussions on non-physical (or what he describes as 'spiritual' and 'moral') aspects of pollutants are marginalised. To obtain a broader philosophical understanding of the nature of Sharia regulations, Fanaei expounds that the Sharia must be understood from a spiritual and moral perspective. He argues that taking recourse to such a perspective can influence the epistemological and hermeneutical interpretation of scriptures (or more specifically, the Qur'an and *ḥadīth* literature) that convey Sharia ordinances. With regards to the impurity of non-Muslims, Fanaei demonstrates that the traditional hermeneutical methodology propounded by Muslim jurists leads them to interpret scripture in a literalistic manner, and as such they dominantly conclude on the physical impurity of non-Muslims. However, a spiritual or moral approach to Sharia gives rise to a hermeneutical method of interpretation that allows scripture to be understood in a symbolic manner. Through giving examples of various scriptural instances, Fanaei expounds that the purpose of Sharia regulations of purity and impurity is simply to remind us that just as the way substances can be contaminated with physical pollutants, human beings (both Muslims and non-Muslims) can be 'symbolically' contaminated with false spiritual and moral values. The former type of contamination requires physical purification, whereas the latter type of contamination requires spiritual and moral purification. He alludes that the natural consequence of taking this approach is that it improves relationships between Muslims and non-Muslims and positively increases interactions between them.

Like Fanaei, Abdul Hussain's contribution is also critical of the dominant interpretive approach taken by Muslim jurists in their deduction of Sharia knowledge. He describes this approach as the mainspring to the non-egalitarian deductions of Sharia regulations of purity and impurity. Abdul Hussain devotes a large part of his study to examining the dominant Shīʿī understanding of the physical impurity of non-Muslims. He commences by clarifying that the juristic notion of non-Muslims being physically impure cannot be located within Sunni *fiqh* nor early Shīʿī *fiqh*. Rather, it is something that only emerged within the precincts of Shīʿī *fiqh* after the fifth/eleventh century onwards. Abdul Hussain's analysis of the matter leads him to the same conclusion as Fanaei, as he suggests that when scripture reveals the impurity of non-Muslims or unbelievers, it must be interpreted in a symbolic manner to indicate their mental impurity (due to false beliefs and values), and must not be interpreted in a literalistic manner to indicate their physical impurity. Abdul Hussain justifies his conclusion by taking recourse to what he terms as the 'existential' approach. The existential approach professes a hermeneutical method of interpretation that distinguishes between the 'essence' and the 'form' of divine ordinances found in the scriptural sources of the Qur'an and *ḥadīth* literature. According to Abdul Hussain, 'essence' refers to universal values that are conveyed in scripture whose efficacy transcends the original context of revelation, whereas 'form' refers to the literal formulation of values that are conveyed in scripture whose efficacy is limited to the context of revelation or a context that is similar (or relatable) to the context of revelation. Abdul Hussain alludes that during the period of revelation it was not easily conceivable to make a hermeneutical distinction between the essence and form of divine ordinances. This is because during the period of revelation, the form, or the formulation of ordinances, lucidly conveyed the essence, or the universal values, intended by God. However, modern socio-economic, political, and technological advancements have contributed toward creating a wide gulf between the original context of revelation and the present-day context. Accordingly, the distinction between the 'essence' and the 'form' of divine ordinances is more pertinent today than ever before. This implies that in today's age the form, or the literal indication, of scripture does not always accurately represent the universal values intended by God. On the basis of this hermeneutical approach, Abdul Hussain attempts to reinterpret (or re-deduce) numerous other Sharia regulations related to purity and impurity that seemingly contrast those that are propounded within the dominant juristic discourse. For instance, he mentions that Sharia only designates substances to be physically impure (such as blood, urine, semen, dead bodies etc.) because they are unhygienic (*khabath*) in themselves; or that the impurity of wine (and any other alcoholic beverage) cannot be directly sourced from scripture, rather scripture (or Sharia) only prohibits its consumption; or that the Sharia permits trading of physically impure substances so long as their utility is conventionally acceptable and they do not sprout any corruption.

The papers presented in this volume represent the multifaceted approach by which scholars and researchers understand and rationalise Sharia regulations of purity and impurity. From the contextual analysis of their origins and compilation to their present-day reception and interpretation(s), this volume expounds the richness and diversity of discussions that emerge from the topic.

This volume demonstrates that *fiqh*, or the human interpretation of Sharia, can be persuaded through various epistemological, theological, and hermeneutical standpoints, and that each standpoint potentially impacts the everyday lives, relationships, and interactions of Muslims in different ways.

On a final note, as guest editor of this volume, I would like to express my sincere appreciation for the hard work and dedication of everyone who has contributed to making the 8th AMI Contemporary Fiqhī Issues Workshop on the Regulations of Purity and Impurity in Islam a success. I specifically would like to thank the speakers, delegates, panel organisers and chairs, who participated in the workshop, and the entire team of AMI, especially Wahid Amin, Muhammed Reza Tajri, Mahdiyah Abdul-Hussain, Rukhsana Bhanji and Ali Redha Khaki.

REZA POURMOHAMMADI

The Role of Purity and Impurity in the Formation of the Muslim Economy in the Early Period of Islam

Unlike other ancient civilizations which were established on riverbanks with the help of a permanent water source, Islamic civilization emerged from arid land.[1] Arabia, the cradle of Islam, did not have sufficient national resources that would serve as a prerequisite for establishing a civilization.[2] It was Islam that played a decisive role in changing the position of Arabia in early history. It transformed its inhabitants, the Arabs, into one nation, by unifying them under one religion and preparing them for a wide series of world conquests. Numerous factors have influenced the formation of Islamic economy and civilization. Undoubtedly one of those factors is the laws of Islam that have led to such an economic system. These law, including contract laws, laws of receiving *zakāt* and *khums*, etc., can be traced throughout Islamic jurisprudence. In this article, I do not intend to discuss all these rulings, but only the rulings related to purity and impurity, and I will try to show their impact on the formation of the Muslim economy. In reading this article, it should be remembered that the present article is just a descriptive and historical study of what has happened in the early period of Islam; it is not trying to explain and understand the reasons for justifying these rulings. For example, I try to understand implications of market rule (*qāʿidat al-sūq*) on the formation of Muslims' economy, but I do not intend, like American legal purposivism, to identify the legislature's purposes to pass these laws, but merely raise the possibility that certain factors may have influenced the formation of the Muslim economy. Furthermore, given the differences of opinion among different schools of Islamic jurisprudence, our focus is on identifying the rulings based on the views of Imāmī school of law.

---

1 I would like to express my gratitude to Ayatollah Modarresi Yazdi for his guidance, and useful critiques of this research work. I would also like to thank Dr. Wahid Amin and Dr. Hashim Bata for their advice and assistance in keeping my progress on schedule, although any errors are my own and should not tarnish the reputations of these esteemed persons. Finally, I would also like to extend my thanks to Al-Mahdi Institute for organizing the workshop.

2 Jawād ʿAlī, *al-Mufaṣṣal fī taʾrīkh al-ʿarab qabl al-islām* (Beirut: Dār al-ʿIlm li-l-Malayīn, 1968), 1:274.

The article proceeds in three parts. In the first part, I briefly explain the economic situation of Muslims in the early days of Islam. By depicting their economic situation at that historical moment, I will be able to better show the effects of economic rulings in the next section. Then, the regulation related to purity and impurity effecting the formation of Muslims' local market will be studied in the second part. Finally, I try to understand and show the result and implications of these rulings on our contemporary economic life as Muslims.

1. The Economic Situation of Muslims in the Early Period of Islam

Since I claim that Islamic rulings, with the help of other factors, have changed the economic situation of Muslims, it is important to have a clear image of the Muslims' economic situation in the early days of Islam. The political strength in the Arabian Peninsula was based on economic strength and it is an undeniable fact that the majority of Muslims were coming from the poorer classes of society.[3] Therefore, they were engaging in and beset with terrible financial difficulties. The income of Muslims in Mecca prior to the migration of the Prophet to Medina was minimal due to Quraysh hostilities and their economic sanctions. During the early years of migration to Medina no significant changes took place in their welfare conditions because these migrations took place in a way so as not to attract the attention of the Quraysh, and almost none of the Muslims could carry any valuable property with them.[4] Many of the migrants could not bring their families, and the new Muslims had to spend their nights on stone benches built around the mosque, as they had no accommodation of their own.[5] Many of these financial problems stemmed from the sanctions imposed on them by the Quraysh, the biggest opposition to Islam at that time.

When Islam began to spread, the Meccans asked Abū Ṭālib (540–619 CE), the uncle and protector of the Prophet, to hand him over to them for execution, but he steadfastly refused. Abū Ṭālib acted fast and called on the members of Banū Hāshim and Banū al-Muṭṭalib to meet at the Kaʿba and convinced them to pledge that they would protect their clansman, Muḥammad. Abū Lahab,

3 Muḥammad b. ʿUmar al-Wāqidī, *Kitab al-maghazi of al-Waqidi*, 3 vols (Oxford: Oxford University Press, 1967), 2:575; Muḥammad Ibn Ḥabīb, *Kitāb al-muḥabbar* (Beirut: Muʾassasat Dār al-Nawādir, 2013), 575; al-Yaʿqūbī, *Tarīkh al-Yaʿqūbī* (Beirut: Dār Ṣādir, 2010), 1:270.

4 Muḥammad b. Jarīr al-Ṭabarī, *The History of al-Ṭabarī: The Foundation of the Community*, trans. M. V. McDonald (New York: State University of New York Press, 1989), 7:8.

5 Ibid., 49.

another of the Prophet's uncles and self-proclaimed sworn enemy, refused to take the pledge and declared he was on the side of the Quraysh.[6] The Quraysh held a meeting and decided to outcast the Banū Hāshim and Banū al-Muṭṭalib by placing them under a total social and economic boycott. The stipulations of this sanction were as follows: other clans from the Quraysh could not marry their daughters, transact business with them, keep company with them, nor would they accept any peaceful overtures from these two clans until they handed over the Prophet. Once all the people present had agreed with the points mentioned above, they put this pact in writing. The Quraysh chiefs signed this document, and the parchment was hung in the Ka'ba to give it authority. This was done on the first of Muharram, in the seventh year of the Prophet's mission.[7] The Prophet, along with Abū Ṭālib and clan members of Banū Hāshim and Banū al-Muṭṭalib, were forced to withdraw from Mecca and live in Valley Abī Ṭālib for two years under severe sanctions, having no access to external trade nor economic relations.[8] The valley rests between Mount Abū Qubays to the south, and Mount Abyaḍ to the north.[9] The boycott was devastating, and for many months they lived in misery. It was so rigorously applied, and food was so scarce, that they had to eat the leaves of trees. The women, and more especially the children and suckling babies, would cry with hunger, which could be heard all over the valley.[10] The Quraysh told the merchants not to sell any goods to them. Prices were increased to prevent them from buying even essentials. They remained in that state for three years. Apart from a few members of the Quraysh who secretly sent food to them, they were totally abandoned. Despite such grim circumstances, the Prophet never ceased inviting non-Muslims to Islam. He was particularly active during the time of Hajj. It was at this time that he would speak to tribes that had travelled to Mecca from all over the Arab world.

---

6 Muḥammad b. Jarīr al-Ṭabarī, *The History of al-Ṭabarī: Muḥammad at Mecca*, trans. W. Montgomery Watt and M. V. McDonald (New York: State University of New York Press, 1988), 6:154.

7 Ibid.

8 'Abd al-Malik Ibn Hishām, *al-Sīra al-nabawiyya* (Dār al-Ma'rifa, 1995), 220.

9 Ibid., 155.

10 Ibid., 155.

2. The Need for Domestic Economy

Considering the economic conditions of the Muslims in the beginning of Islam, it can be concluded that any kind of effort in formation and support of the Muslims' economy was in fact a trial for survival. The important question to be asked here is: what are the first steps in creating and supporting an economy? It is an unquestionable fact in economic studies that the first step towards establishing a strong and independent economy is first to create a strong and dynamic domestic economy, or what is called the 'Inner-city Economy'. Economists consider two basic principles for establishing any domestic economy:[11] (1) Buy your own products: strengthen existing and emerging inner-city clusters (clusters are basically the network of small businesses that support each other such as food wholesalers and restaurant owners), and increase company recognition and strengthen business networks. Honouring the work of small businesses is more than just flattery, and it actually helps build connections with other similar businesses and fuels competition; (2) keep money in the community: when money is spent locally it can be re-spent locally, raising the overall level of economic activity, paying more salaries, and building the local tax base. This re-circulating of money leads to an increase in economic activity, with the degree of expanse entirely dependent on the percentage of money spent locally.[12]

11 See Michael E. Porter, 'Inner-City Economic Development: Learnings From 20 Years of Research and Practice', *Economic Development Quarterly* 30, no. 2 (May 1, 2016):105–16; Bob Sutcliffe, 'Industry and Underdevelopment Re-examined', *The Journal of Development Studies* 21, no. 1 (October 1, 1984): 121–33; Robert B. Sutcliffe and Robert Baldwin Sutcliffe, *Industry and Underdevelopment* (Addison-Wesley, 1971); Felipe Pazos, 'Have Import Substitution Policies Either Precipitated or Aggravated the Debt Crisis?', *Journal of Interamerican Studies and World Affairs* 27, no. 4 (1985):57–73; Eqbal Al-Rahmani, 'Economic Independence: Concepts and Strategies, a Theoretical Investigation and an Empirical Case Study', *Doctoral Dissertations*, (January 1, 1988), 25; Albert O. Hirschman, 'A Generalized Linkage Approach to Development, with Special Reference to Staples', in *The Essential Hirschman*, ed. Jeremy Adelman (Princeton: Princeton University Press, 2013), 14.

12 Simon Hornblower and Antony Spawforth, *The Oxford Companion to Classical Civilization* (Oxford: Oxford University Press, 2003), 51–57.

The Muslims' independence, in general, is one of the values that many verses of the Qur'an and *ḥadīths* emphasize.[13] For instance, the Qur'an says: 'God will never provide the faithless any way [to prevail] over the faithful.'[14] Economic self-sufficiency and independence, in verses and narrations, are introduced as one of the intentions of Islamic government.[15] The Qur'an considers independence and the potency of Islamic society as a value, and prevents Muslims from abjection and dependence on enemies. For instance, as the Qur'an expounds: 'Prepare against them whatever you can of [military] power.'[16] And: 'God will never provide the faithless any way [to prevail] over the faithful.'[17] I do not want to convince you here that the first step in the formation of any economy is to create an independent and domestic economy. I leave the proof of this presupposition to our respected economists, but I assure you that this presupposition is considered relatively axiomatic in all economic schools.[18] In future arguments, I will discuss how the Prophet stipulated rules and regulations on the subject of purity and impurity, resulting in the strong and local economic formation among Muslims. In the following section, I endeavour to demonstrate the rulings related to purity and impurity, which have led to the formation of the domestic economy among Muslims.

3. Purity and Impurity Regulations Forming the Muslims' Inner-Economy

As I explained in the introduction, rulings affecting the formation of the Muslim economy fall into several categories:

(1) Some Islamic rulings have clearly influenced the formation of the Muslim economy, but have nothing to do with purity and impurity regulation. For instance: (a) Investment partnerships (*al-muḍāraba*) between Muslims and non-Muslims is discouraged (*makrūh*), especially if a dealer is a non-Muslim.[19]

---

13 Abū Ja'far Muḥammad b. Ya'qūb al-Kulaynī, *al-Kāfī* (Tehran: Dār al-Kutub al-Islāmiyya, 1407 AH), 5:74.

14 Qur'an 4:141.

15 Qur'an 4:141.

16 Qur'an 8:25.

17 Ibid., 4:141.

18 See footnote 12.

19 al-Kulaynī, *al-Kāfī*, 5:286; Muḥammad b. 'Ali b. Bābawayh al-Qummī (Ibn Bābawayh), *Man lā yaḥḍuruhu al-faqīh* (Qum: Islamic Publication Institute, 1984), 3:408; Muḥam-

Undoubtedly, this ruling leads to the greater use of Muslim human resources. (b) There is no usury (*ribā*) in dealings between Muslims and warring disbelievers (*kāfir al-ḥarb*). But it is permissible in dealings between a Muslim and a *dhimmi* (a disbeliever enjoying Muslim protection).[20] Consider that usury is known as one of the most destructive activities for economies, which is banned in many legal systems of the world.[21] Permission to receive interest from non-Muslims actually weakens the economic system of non-Muslims and strengthens the economic system of Muslims. (c) There is consensus that a non-Muslim will not inherit from a Muslim. Hence neither a *dhimmi* nor a warring disbeliever (*kāfir al-ḥarb*) can inherit from a Muslim, while a Muslim inherits from a non-Muslim.[22] (d) The creation of a *waqf* (specific kind of donation) in favour of a *ḥarbī* is not valid, even if he is a blood relative.[23]

(2) Some rulings have influenced the formation of the Muslim domestic economy and are related to purity and impurity, such as the impurity of skin slaughtered by a non-Muslim, or the impurity of milk and water that has been in contact with the body of a non-Muslim. In the present study, my main aim is to convince you that these rulings directly or indirectly impacted the formation of the domestic economy among Muslims. There are many such rulings, but I will discuss the main ones below.

---

mad b. al-Ḥasan b. ʿAlī b. al-Ḥasan al-Ṭūsī, *Tahdhīb al-aḥkām* (Qum: Dār al-Kutub al-Islāmiyya, 1986), 7:185; al-Ḥasan b. Yūsuf b. ʿAlī b. al-Muṭahhar al-Ḥillī, *Tadhkirat al-fuqahā* (Qum: Āl al-Bayt Institite, 1993), 2:221; Muḥammad Kāẓim Yazdī, *al-ʿUrwat al-wuthqā* (Qum: Islamic Publication Institute, 2000), 271.

20 See Qur'an 4:141. See also Jaʿfar b. al-Ḥasan b. Yaḥyā (al-Muḥaqqiq al-Ḥillī), *Sharāʾiʿ al-islām fī masāʾil al-ḥalāl wa-l-ḥarām* (Qum: Ismailian Publication, 1987), 1:157; Muḥammad Bāqir b. Muḥammad Taqī Majlisī, *Biḥār al-anwār al-jāmiʿa li-durar akhbār al-aʾimmat al-aṭhār* (Qum: Dār Iḥyāʾ al-Turāth al-ʿArabī, 1982), 39:47; Muḥammad b. al-Ḥasan b. ʿAlī b. al-Ḥusayn al-Ḥurr al-ʿĀmilī, *Tafṣīl wasāʾil al-shīʿa ilā taḥṣīl masāʾil al-sharīʿa* (Qum: Āl al-Bayt Institite, 1995), 17:376; Mirzā Ḥusayn Nūrī, *Mustadrak al-wasāʾil* (Qum: Āl al-Bayt Institute, 1987), 17:142; Ibn Bābawayh, *Man lā yaḥḍuruhū l-faqīh*, 4:243.

21 See M. Siddieq Noorzoy, 'Islamic Laws on Riba (Interest) and Their Economic Implications', *International Journal of Middle East Studies* 14, no. 1 (1982):3–17.

22 al-Muhaqqiq al-Hilli, *Sharāʾiʿ al-islām*, 4: 165; al-Ḥurr al-ʿAmilī, *Tafṣīl wasāʾil al-shīʿa*, 26:327; Abū Bakr al-Sarakhsī, *Kitāb al-mabsūṭ* (Beirut: Dār al-Maʿrifa, 1978), 30:30.

23 al-Ḥillī, *Tadhkirat al-fuqahā*, 2:429.

3.1 Regulations Related to the Prohibition of Animal Products Slaughtered by Non-Muslims

In the Arabian Peninsula, due to high temperatures and sparse rainfall, cultivation did not take place.[24] However, in other scattered valleys and low yielding pastures it was possible for other tribes to live nomadic lives and breed livestock.[25] Therefore, breeding cows, sheep, camel, and horses were the main economic activity prevailing in those days.[26] Camels were preferred to other livestock; this was due to the camel's diversified range of by-products (such as milk, wool, meat) and its ability to feed on low-grade pastures and tolerance to feed shortage. Furthermore, the camel has various uses in transportation, wars, and animal breeding, and, finally, has the benefit of a longer life span compared with other animals. Horses were used mostly in wars for battle and for swift escapes. Sheep were very delicate, and cows could not be transferred to mountainous and impassable pastures; also, they could not graze in low-grade meadows. As reported, during the reign of the Prophet, a number of people were employed in weaving, sewing, and leatherwear. As is evident, all these trades are based on animal products.[27]

24 Melinda A. Zedler, Daniel G. Bradley, Eve Emshwiller, and Bruce D. Smith (eds.), *Documenting Domestication: New Genetic and Archaeological Paradigms*, 1st ed. (University of California Press, 2006); Melinda A. Zeder, 'The Origins of Agriculture in the Near East', *Current Anthropology* 52, no. S4 (October 1, 2011):S221–35.

25 Medina, Ṭā'if, Khaybar, Ḥunayn, Wādī al-Qurā and Yemen were the exceptional regions in the Arabian Peninsula that could support agricultural activity due to adequate rainfall. For this reason, cultivation, planting trees and animal husbandry were among the particular activities of the inhabitants of Medina. The main agricultural products of Medina were dates, grapes, figs, wheat and barley. Cultivation of perishable crops and vegetables was also customary here and there.

26 See Paula Wapnish and Brian Hesse, 'Urbanization and the Organization of Animal Production at Tell Jemmeh in the Middle Bronze Age Levant', *Journal of Near Eastern Studies* 47, no. 2 (1988):81–94; Jean-Denis Vigne et al., 'Predomestic Cattle, Sheep, Goat and Pig during the Late 9th and the 8th Millennium Cal. BC on Cyprus: Preliminary Results of Shillourokambos (Perkklisha, Limassol)', *Archaeozoology of the Near East* IV, (January 1, 2000), 52–75; Roger Blench and Kevin MacDonald (eds.), *The Origins and Development of African Livestock: Archaeology, Genetics, Linguistics and Ethnography*, 1st edition (London: Routledge, 2011); Sue Colledge et al. (eds.), *The Origins and Spread of Domestic Animals in Southwest Asia and Europe*, 1st edition (Walnut Creek, California: Routledge, 2013).

27 Muḥammad b. Ja'far al-Kattānī and S. Z Chowdhury, *al-Arba'īn: On the Duty of Loving the Noble Family of the Prophet Muhammad* (London: Turath Publishing, 2010), 2:103.

Tazkiya is the Arabic term for the correct method regarding the slaughter of animals according to the requirements of the Islamic law.[28] This method is an act of faith, and it is necessary for the slaughter of all animals and birds, the meat of which has been made permissible for human consumption.[29] It is important to note that products from animals in the early period of Islam include meat, butter, oil, clothing, shoes, scabbard, writing materials, etc.[30] It is forbidden for a non-Muslim to slaughter an animal himself, and if he does it, the slaughtered animal will be considered as a dead animal (*al-mayta*) for Muslims which they cannot consume.[31] Hence, slaughtered animals of non-Muslims, including Jews, Christians, and Magians, are unlawful to eat.[32] The Qur'an expounds upon this, saying: 'Say (you, Muhammad): find nothing in what has been revealed to me that forbids men to eat of any food except carrion, spilt blood, swine flesh, for these are unclean, or an abomination over which a name other than that of God had been invoked.'[33] And, 'He (God) has forbidden you carrion, blood, swine flesh and that (meat) over which a name other than that of God has been invoked.'[34] And, 'You are forbidden (the consumption] of carrion, blood, swine flesh, that (meat] over which a name other than that of God has been invoked, [the meat of] strangled animals, those that have fallen, been beaten or rammed (or gorged by other animals) to death, those mangled (or devoured) by beasts of prey, save those which you slaughter in time, and those sacrificed to idols.'[35] Shīʿīs, however, come to regard all acts

28 Muḥammad b. Mukarram b. Manẓūr, *Lisān al-ʿarab* (Beirut: Dār al-Kutub al-ʿIlmiyya, 2006), 14:288; al-Khalīl b. Aḥmad al-Farāhīdī, *Kitāb al-ʿayn* (Bagdad: Dār al-Rashīd Li-l-Nashr, 1980), 5:339; Aḥmad b. Muḥammad al-Fayyūmī, *Kitāb miḍyāḥ al-munīr fī gharīb al-sharḥ al-kabīr li-l-rifāʿī* (Beirut: al-Maṭbaʿa al-Amīriyya, 1920), 2:209.

29 Muḥammad b. al-Ḥasan b. ʿAlī b. al-Ḥasan al-Ṭūsī, *al-Istibṣār fīmā ukhtulifa min al-akhbār* (Qum: Dār al-Kutub al-Islāmiyya, 2011), 4:40; al-Ṭūsī, *Tahdhīb al-aḥkām*, 9:65; al-Muḥaqqiq al-Ḥillī, *Sharāʾiʿ al-islām*, 3:159; al-Kulayni, *al-Kāfī*, 6:238; Muḥsin Fayḍ Kāshānī, *al-Wāfī* (Qum: Imam Ali Publication, 1985), 6:238; Sayyid ʿAlī b. Muḥammad ʿAli Ṭabāṭabāʾī, *Rīyāḍ al-masāʾil fī bayān al-aḥkām bi-l-dalāʾil* (Qum: Dār Iḥyāʾ al-Turāth al-ʿArabī, 2009), 2:270; Zayn al-Dīn al-ʿĀmilī (al-Shahīd al-Thānī), *Masālik al-afhām fī sharḥ sharāʾiʿ al-islām* (Qum: Islamic Knowledge Society, 1992), 11:454.

30 Ibid.

31 Ṭabāṭabāʾī, *Rīyāḍ al-masāʾil*, 2:270; al-Shahīd al-Thānī, *Masālik al-afhām*, 11:454.

32 According to one narration, it is permissible to eat the sacrifice slaughtered by a *dhimmi* if his *tasmiya* (mentioning God's Name) is heard, but this view is out of date nowadays.

33 Qur'an 6:145.

34 Qur'an 6:173.

35 Qur'an 5:3.

of ritual slaughter performed by non-Muslims as invalid. This prohibition of animal products slaughtered by non-Muslims is not based on the notion that non-Muslims are impure (*najis*), but rather on the assertion that non-Muslim butchers are incapable of fulfilling the requirement to invoke God's name during the act of slaughter.[36]

3.2 Regulations Related to the Prohibition of Water, Beverages, and Moist Foodstuffs

Every liquid in which one of the impure (*najis*) substances is mixed, such as blood or urine or excrement, is prohibited if the mixing occurs when it is in a liquid state, even if it is of large quantity since there is no way to purify it.[37] But if it is in a solid state and an impure substance falls into it while solid, such as hard treacle, cooking butter, and honey, the impurity can be removed and the upper layer containing it has to be erased, when the rest will be permissible (*ḥalāl*) to eat.[38] If the liquid is fat (oil), it is permissible to use it for lighting in an open space but not under a shed.[39] The same rule is applied to every oil in which an animal whose blood gushes out. Since non-Muslims themselves are considered impure (*najis*)[40], any liquid they handle or touch with their bare hands becomes impure too, whether they be *ḥarbi* or *dhimmi*s, as per a more

36 Muḥammad b. al-Ḥasan b. ʿAlī b. al-Ḥasan al-Ṭūsī, *al-Mabsūṭ fī fiqh al-Imāmīyya* (al-Maktaba al-Murtaẓawiyya, 1967), 7:289; Ṭabāṭabā'ī, *Rīyāḍ al-masā'il*, 2:270.

37 al-Muḥaqqiq al-Ḥillī, *Sharā'iʿ al-islām*, 1:4; Muḥammad Ḥasan al-Najafī, *Jawāhir al-kalām fī sharḥ sharā'iʿ al-islām* (Qum: Institute of Encyclopedia of Islamic Jurisprudence Publications, 2000), 1:71; Murtaḍā b. Muḥammad Amīn al-Anṣārī (al-Shaykh al-Anṣārī), *Kitāb al-ṭahāra* (Qum: Majmaʿ al-Fikr al-Islāmī, n.d.), 1:68.

38 al-Muḥaqqiq al-Ḥillī, *Sharā'iʿ al-islām*, 1:4; Muḥammad Ḥasan al-Najafī, *Jawāhir al-kalām*, 1:71; al-Shaykh al-Anṣārī, *Kitāb al-ṭahāra*, 1:68.

39 Muḥammad Ḥasan al-Najafī, *Jawāhir al-kalām*, 9:22; al-Shaykh al-Anṣārī, *Kitāb al-ṭahāra*, 1:8.

40 See Qur'an 9:28, 6:125. See also Abū l-Qāsim Najm al-Dīn, *Sharā'iʿ al-islām fī masā'il al-ḥalāl wa-l-ḥarām* (Qum: Ismailian Publication, 1987): 1:45; Muḥammad Ḥasan al-Najafī, *Jawāhir al-kalām*, 6:41; al-Sayyid Muḥammad b. ʿAli al-Mūsawī al-ʿĀmilī, *Jāmiʿ al-madārik fī sharḥ al-mukhtaṣar al-nāfiʿ* (Qum: Maktabat al-Ṣadūq, 1976), 2:294; Najm al-Dīn Abū l-Qāsim Jaʿfar b. al-Ḥasan b. Yaḥyā b. al-Ḥasan b. Saʿīd, *al-Muʿtabar fī sharḥ al-mukhtaṣar* (Sayed al-Shuhada Institite, 1985), 1:440.

widely held opinion.[41] Furthermore, using the utensils they have used for liquids is not permissible.[42] The majority of Shīʿī jurists hold that the impurity of non-Muslims is communicable through contact with Muslims and with water, beverages, and moist foodstuffs.[43] Therefore, the preparation of bread and dairy products like milk, yogurt, cream, butter, cheese, casein, involves contact with moist foodstuffs susceptible to contracting communicable forms of impurity.[44] Al-Mufīd states that: 'This impurity is communicable to Muslims through direct contact, apparently on the grounds that the sweat of a non-Muslim is impure; sweat, a form of *su'r*, bears the same purity status as its source.'[45]

3.3 Regulations Related to the Prohibition of Wine and Pork

As explained earlier, the types of rulings on the formation of the domestic economy can be divided into two categories: rulings with direct impact; and rulings with indirect impact. 'Rulings with direct effects' are rulings that directly establish and strengthen the domestic economy among Muslims, while 'rulings with indirect effects' are rulings that indirectly support the Muslim economy by weakening an opponent's economy. For example, consider China as the trade rival of Germany. Sometimes by stipulating certain rules, Germany supports local production. This is the direct support that should be considered as the first kind. But sometimes Germany bans the import of certain goods from China. In the latter scenario, Germany is helping to strengthen its own economy by weakening its rival economy. I believe that some of the rulings on purity and impurity belong to the latter group, which has helped the Muslim economy by weakening the rival economy. In order to prove that the impurity of wine and pork has really weakened the non-Muslim market, it is important to know the centrality of wine and pork in the non-Muslim market.

---

41 Muḥammad Kāẓim Yazdī, *al-ʿUrwat al-wuthqā*, 1:73; Sayyid Rūḥallāh Khumaynī, *Taḥrīr al-wasīla* (Institute for Compilation and Publication of Imam Khomeini's Works, 2013), 1:40.

42 al-Ḥurr al-ʿAmilī, *Tafṣīl wasāʾil al-shīʿa*, 16:475; 1:159. It is reported that if a Muslim person wants to make a Magian his messmate (share with him in dining), he is required to order him to wash his hands, but this opinion is obsolete.

43 Muḥammad Kāẓim Yazdī, *al-ʿUrwat al-wuthqā*, 1:73; Sayyid Rūḥallāh Khumaynī, *Tahrīr al-wasīla*, 1:40.

44 See al-ʿAllāma al-Ḥillī, *Tadhkirat al-fuquhāʾ*, 2:1026.

45 Muḥammad b. al-Nuʿmān al-Mufīd, *al-Muqniʿa* (Qum: Islamic Publication Institute, 1989), 65.

Wine was very common in Arabia before Islam.[46] Some modern Arabic authors maintain that there are approximately 1,000 words for wine beverages in Arabic, while others claim only 250 words. Ibn Sīdah, in his book *al-Mukhaṣṣaṣ*, collected about 100 names for wine. These words are to be found in Arabic lexica and in different Arabic classical authors.[47] The variety of the nomenclature of wine in Arabic indicates that wine was an essential part of the daily life and culture of the Arabs. Apart from this linguistic analysis, there are many other evidences for the centrality of wine in Arab culture.[48] Interestingly, the word trader (*tājir*) has meant the wine-seller by some scholars.[49] This usage clearly shows the role of wine in the Arab (specifically the Quraysh tribe) economy. Regarding the sanctity of wine, the Qur'an expounds that: 'They ask you about wine and gambling. Say, in them is great sin and [yet, some] benefit for people. But their sin is greater than their benefit.'[50] Therefore, when Islam declares this central commodity impure, what destructive effects this religious ruling has had on the economy of the Quraysh is quite predictable.

Pork was considered one of the basic commodities in the non-Muslim market in the early period of Islam.[51] Pork meat at this time was an extremely common food in Arabian Peninsula and, as far as we know, was not banned or eschewed by any particular group. In fact, in several of these early cultures, pigs actually had a religious significance. For example, both the ancient Greeks and Old Kingdom Egyptians sacrificed pigs to a variety of deities. Regarding the sanctity of pork, the Qur'an expounds that: 'Prohibited to you are dead animals, blood, the flesh of swine, except what you [are able to] slaughter [before

46 W. Montgomery Watt and M. V. McDonald, trans., *The History of al-Ṭabarī* (Albany, NY: State University of New York Press, 1987), 6: 20, 34, 36, 48, 84.

47 Muḥammad b. Ya'qūb Fīrūzābādī, *al-Qāmūs al-muḥīṭ* (Qum: Resalah Publishing, 2015), 301.

48 Watt and McDonald, *The History of al-Ṭabarī*, 6:20, 34, 36, 48, 84.

49 Sayyid 'Abd al-Ḥusayn Lārī, *Majmu'a rasā'il* (Qum: Lari Congress, 1997), 309.

50 Qur'an 2:219.

51 See Seyyed Hossein Nasr, *An Introduction to Islamic Cosmological Doctrines*, Rev ed. (Albany: State University of New York Press, 1993), 70; Richard W. Redding, 'The Pig and the Chicken in the Middle East: Modeling Human Subsistence Behavior in the Archaeological Record Using Historical and Animal Husbandry Data', *Journal of Archaeological Research* 23, no. 4 (December 1, 2015): 325–68; Marvin Harris, *The Sacred Cow and the Abominable Pig: Riddles of Food and Culture* (New York: Touchstone Books, 1987).

its death].'[52] Imām Muḥammad al-Bāqir, addressing a query about dishes or cookware belonging to non-Muslims, declares: 'Do not eat from them when [their owners] have eaten carrion, blood, or pork from them.'[53] Also, he prohibits the use of non-Muslim vessels that previously contained wine.[54] Imām Ja'far al-Ṣādiq prohibits the consumption of food associated with *ahl al-kitāb* on the grounds that 'wine and pork are in their dishes.'[55]

3.4 The Market Rule (*qā'idat al-sūq*)

Whatever is sold in the markets of the Muslims, including sacrifices (slaughtered animals) and all sorts of meat, is pure and permissible to purchase, and there is no need to investigate and inquire about its state.[56] Various authentic narrations permit the consumption of meat and related products found in the Muslim marketplace whose preparation may not conform to Islamic norms.[57] In this regard, Fuḍayl, Muḥammad b. Muslim, and Zurāra b. A'yan asked Imām Muḥammad al-Bāqir about purchasing meat from the Muslim market, and he responded: 'If it has been purchased from the Muslim market, eat it and do not ask about its purity.'[58] In some narrations, the cause is mentioned, expressing that if such a rule did not exist, Muslim marketing and trade would be suspended, which the lawgiver abominates.[59] Also, according to the market rule, meat or skin that is purchased from the non-Muslim market, even if it was probably slaughtered by Muslims, but we are not sure, is known as *najis*. The role of this rule, which all jurisprudential schools agree on, is unquestionable information and support of the Muslims' market.

---

52 Qur'an 5:3.

53 al-Ḥurr al-'Āmilī, *Tafṣīl wasā'il al-shī'a*, 24: 211.

54 Ibid., 206.

55 Ibid.

56 al-Ḥurr al-'Āmilī, *Tafṣīl wasā'il al-shī'a*, 16:475; 3:490–426; Abū Ḥanīfa al-Nu'mān b. Muḥammad, *Da'ā'im al-islām wa-dhikr al-ḥalāl wa-l-ḥarām* (Cairo: Dār al-Ma'ārif, 1965), 2:126; al-Mufīd, *al-Muqni'a*, 580; Abū Ja'far Muḥammad b. Ḥasan al-Ṭūsī, *al-Istibṣār*, 3:85; idem, *Tahdhīb al-aḥkām*, 7:83.

57 Ibid.

58 Abū Ja'far Muḥammad b. Ḥasan al-Ṭūsī, *Tahdhīb al-aḥkām*, 9:72, 306–307.

59 al-Kulaynī, *al-Kāfī*, 7:387. See also al-Shaykh Yusūf al-Baḥrānī, *al-Hadā'iq al-nāḍira* (Qum: Islamic Publication, 1992), 5:64.

4. Purity and Impurity Regulation and Muslims' Contemporary Economy

So far, I have explained the role of purity and impurity regulations on the formation of the Muslims' domestic economy. The question I want to answer in this section is: what is the role of purity and impurity regulations on our contemporary world and contemporary economy? In other words, what effects do those rulings have on the Muslim economy today? How does it affect the economic life of Muslims directly or indirectly? The 2019–20 State of the Global Islamic Economy report estimates that Muslims spent $2.2 trillion in 2018 across the food, pharmaceutical, and lifestyle sectors that are impacted by Islamic faith-inspired ethical consumption needs.[60] This spending reflects a healthy 5.2% year-on-year growth and is forecasted to reach $3.2 trillion by 2024 at a Cumulative Annual Growth Rate (CAGR) of 6.2%. In addition, Islamic finance assets were reported to have reached $2.5 trillion in 2018.[61] Many of these markets benefit from purity and impurity regulations, for example, markets such as Halal Food, Halal Travel, Modest Fashion, Halal Pharmaceuticals, Halal Cosmetics. Although the purity and impurity regulations impact many markets, in the following I focus specifically on its role on the Muslims' food market, which is almost the largest market affected by these regulation.[62] Halal food has rapidly expanded beyond ritually slaughtered permissible meat. The sector has had to expand its Halal-certified offerings, in line with the global nature of the food production chain, with ingredients no longer sourced solely from local producers but invariably from multiple locations. Globally Muslims spend on food an estimated $1.37 trillion in 2018, growing at 5.1% from 2017. Spending is forecast to grow by 6.3% per year to reach $2.0 trillion by 2024.[63] As the food production chain has changed, Muslims have had to pay heightened attention to the labelling of products across the value chain, with concerns spanning non-ritually slaughtered meat to porcine gelatine, additives, and colourings. It was to reassure Muslim consumers, as well as to drive sales, that global candy manufacturers Haribo, Nestlé and Ferrero Rocher acquired Halal certification. Such attention to labels and the origins of food products is increasingly apparent among Muslim and non-Muslim consumers alike as they browse store shelves around the world. The Halal

60 Dinar Standard, 'State of the Global Islamic Economy Report 2019-20', 2020, 2.

61 Ibid., 2.

62 Ibid., 29–147.

63 Ibid., 29–53.

food sector is well-positioned to ride the cusp of the labelling and traceability wave. Trust, ethics, and traceability are integral to Halal food, which needs to not only be permissible, but wholesome, pure, and clean. As a result, while more food companies are getting Halal-certification, they are also being certified as organic as well as touting their ethical commitments, including companies such as UK-based Pronto Eat.[64]

Halal food companies are increasingly adapting to the changing realities of the market, yet there is significant potential for more to be done. Halal-certification continues to remain fragmented throughout the world, with sustainability not yet a core component of the certifying process. Initiatives are underway to better unify global Halal trade, such as through the Dubai-based International Halal Accreditation Forum (IHAF) and Malaysia's International Halal Accreditation Board (IHAB). Malaysia and Indonesia are also working more closely on Halal standards, driven in part by Indonesia's decision to require all domestic production of food and related products and services, as well as imports, to be Halal-certified.[65] However established this sector becomes, there seems to always be further room for growth and opportunity. For example, there has recently been a rise in Halal online meal takeout and delivery platforms, particularly in non-OIC countries. The UK-based HalalEat, Halalonclick in Singapore, and the Russian HalalEda.me are just a few examples that also highlight the transnational potential of the Halal Food sector.[66] Several notable private equity investments have occurred in the past year, signalling increasing investor appetite for Halal food investments. ESP Capital and Kingsley Capital Partners invested $30 million in Janan Meat, a leading UK-based Halal lamb and mutton supplier, while Abraaj Capital and Texas Pacific Group invested $400 million in Saudi Arabia-based, fast-food chain Kudu.[67]

Unfortunately, there remains much misunderstanding around Halal meat within non-Muslim majority societies. Some European countries have even moved to ban Halal and Kosher methods of slaughter. To create a better understanding of the principles of Halal food, further funding and work is needed in marketing and sales.[68] Nevertheless, the Halal food sector's growth shows no sign of slowing down, as this report estimates Muslim food and beverage

64 Ibid., 31.
65 Ibid., 35.
66 Ibid.
67 Ibid., 42–47.
68 Ibid., 46.

expenditure to grow to $1.9 trillion by 2021. With creative innovations taking place such as the Ramadan Energy Bar and many opportunities to tap into high potential segments such as Halal baby food, the Halal food sector proves it will remain flourishing for many years to come.[69]

Conclusion

Among the laws of Islam, there are many rulings that directly or indirectly help the Muslim economy. In this article, I have tried to show the impact of some of these rulings, specifically purity and impurity regulations, on the formation and support of Muslims' markets, and how these rulings have been effective in realizing the idea of the inner-city economy. Finally, using some statistical research, I tried to trace the implications of these rulings on the Muslim economy in the contemporary world, and I came to the conclusion that these rulings have controlled a large amount of capital to be exchanged annually only among Muslims.

69 Ibid., 52.

STEPHEN BURGE

The Structure and Message of al-Kulaynī's *Book of Purity*: A Modern Reading of a Classical Text

Whereas religious rituals are events that occur at specific moments in time and often in specific places, questions of ritual purity permeate daily life as sources of ritual pollution are easily encountered throughout the course of a day. Scholars in Islamic studies have highlighted the fact that in contrast to other purity systems, such as those of Zoroastrianism and Judaism, Islam generally has a more relaxed attitude to ritual pollution.[1] For example, Kevin Reinhart has argued that Sunnī legal works are only concerned with an individual's impurity and contact with pollutants at the moment a ritual action is about to be performed;[2] and Brannon Wheeler has shown that Muslim legal works are generally unconcerned with the presence of pollutants such as urine and semen, which are easily purified.[3] However, the legal works that Wheeler and Reinhart discussed do not reveal the whole picture: outside Sunnī legal works concerns around individuals coming into contact with pollutants are much greater. For example, there are several *ḥadīth* (traditions) that state that the angel that records an individual's words and actions is absent when a person is impure or is in the presence of pollutants: this has a significant impact on an individual's personal eschatological status, since in the presence of polluting substances an individual cannot perform any deeds that would be credited to them in the afterlife. In effect the *ḥadīth* literature often advocates perpetual purity, rather than purity only being a concern during the performance of rituals, as legal works argue.[4] This suggests that there is an important disjunction between the legal positions of the jurists and the broader spirituality of purity found in *ḥadīth* literature.

1 E.g. Ze'ev Maghen, *After Hardship, Cometh Ease: The Jews as Backdrop for Muslim Moderation* (Berlin: De Gruyter, 2006).
2 Kevin A Reinhart, 'Impurity/no danger', *History of Religions* 30 (1990): 1–24.
3 Brannon Wheeler, 'Touching the Penis in Islamic Law', *History of Religions* 44 (2004): 89–119.
4 S. R. Burge, 'Impurity / Danger!' *Islamic Law and Society* 17 (2010): 320–349. See also Richard Gauvain, *Salafi Ritual Purity: In the Presence of God* (London: Routledge, 2013).

The study of ritual theory and purity in Islam has focused on Sunnī approaches,[5] with Shīʿī thought having been largely neglected. The studies of Sunnī ritual purity do, however, highlight the differences between formal legal (i.e. *fiqhī*) discussions on purity and positions found in *ḥadīth* literature. Given the importance of Prophetic *ḥadīth* and the *akhbār* (narrations) of the Imāms in the formulation of Shīʿī law, it is important to consider the position taken in collections of *ḥadīth* and *akhbār* on ritual purity and the spirituality that they espouse. This chapter will look at one particular collection of *ḥadīth* and *akhbār*, namely the *Kitāb al-ṭahāra* from al-Kulaynī's *al-Kāfī fī ʿilm al-dīn*, to explore how ritual purity is understood in one collection of Shīʿī *akhbār*.

The *al-Kāfī* of Abū Jaʿfar Muḥammad b. Yaʿqūb al-Kulaynī (d. 329/940–941) is one of the most important collections of Shīʿī *akhbār*, yet both its author and the work itself remain largely understudied in Western academia with very few monographs and articles devoted to either al-Kulaynī or the *al-Kāfī*.[6] The *Furūʿ al-Kāfī*, which deals with legal issues, has received even less attention, although Robert Gleave has made a short comparative study of the chapters on *tayammum*.[7] Indeed, most of the scholarly interest in al-Kulaynī has focused on the first portion of his *al-Kāfī*, which discusses key theological ideas such as the Imamate.[8] This brief chapter will, in no way, be able to provide a detailed understanding of al-Kulaynī's legal thought or his methods of compilation, but

5 Marion Holmes Katz, *Body of Text: The Emergence of the Sunnī Law of Ritual Purity* (Albany: State University of New York Press, 2002); Ze'ev Maghen, *Virtues of the Flesh: Passion and Purity in Early Islamic Jurisprudence* (Leiden: Brill, 2005).

6 One important example is Muhammad Ismail Marcinkowski, 'Al-Kulayni and his Early Twelver Shīʿite Ḥadīth Collection', *Islamic Culture* 74 (2000): 89–126. See also Saiyad Nizamuddin Ahmad, 'Twelver Šīʿī *ḥadīth*: From Tradition to Contemporary Evaluations', *Oriente Moderno* 82 (2002): 125–145; and Ron P. Buckley, 'On the Origins of Shīʿī Ḥadīth', *The Muslim World* 88 (1998): 165–184.

7 Robert Gleave discusses parts of al-Kulaynī's *Kitāb al-ṭahāra* briefly in his 'Between *Hadīth* and *Fiqh*: The "Canonical" Imāmī Collections of *akhbār*', *Islamic Law and Society* 8 (2001): 350–382, at 356–359.

8 Muhammad A. Amir-Moezzi, *Le prevue de Dieu: la mystique shi'ite à travers l'oeuvre de Kulaynī, IXe-Xe siècle* (Paris: Les éditions du Cerf, 2018); Andrew Newman, *The Formative Period of Twelver Shīʿism: Hadīth as Discourse between Qum and Baghdad* (Richmond: Curzon, 2000), 94–112; Tamima Bayhom Daou, 'The Imāmī Shīʿī Conception of Knowledge of the Imām and Sources of Religious Doctrine in the Formative Period: From Hishām b. al-Ḥakam (d. 179 A.H.) to Kulīnī (d. 329 A.H.)' (PhD. Thesis, School of Oriental and African Studies, University of London, 1996); Georges Vajda, 'Aperçu sur le K. al-Tauḥīd d'al-Kulīnī', *Acta Orientalia* 12 (1961): 231–234.

it is hoped that by exploring one chapter of the *Furūʿ al-Kāfī* in detail, it will be possible to shed some light on Shīʿī *akhbār* on purity and al-Kulaynī's own positions on it. Given that *akhbār* remain important in modern legal thought and in contemporary spirituality, al-Kulaynī's contribution to the debates regarding ritual purity will be invaluable.

This chapter will approach al-Kulaynī's *Kitāb al-ṭahāra* using the method of compilation criticism. This methodology of reading *ḥadīth* collections explores the ways in which *ḥadīth* and *akhbār* have been compiled in order to unearth the underlying thinking that contributed to the form and structure of a collection. Andrew Newman argues in his *Formative Period of Twelver Shīʿism* that the way in which a compiler puts a collection together reveals something of the way they were thinking and which ideas they were seeking to emphasise. As a compiler of *ḥadīth*, there is no ability to control the content of the *ḥadīth* themselves (i.e. the *matan*), but a compiler is able to make decisions about which *ḥadīth* to include and how to arrange them. The decision to include and exclude is a key component in a compiler's ability to control meaning and to articulate a broader discourse.[9] This is not something that is only seen in *ḥadīth* collections, but Norman Calder has noted the importance and power of choice in the writing of *tafsīr*: some exegetes 'hide' potential interpretations to emphasize other ideas.[10] The same power in choice can be found in *ḥadīth* collections too, which is one of the main ideas that Andrew Newman argues is seen in the formative collections of Shīʿī *akhbār*.[11]

The extent to which the act of arrangement can influence the meaning and interpretation of a compilation can also be seen in an important study of Louis Pouzet in which he compared and contrasted two *arbaʿūn* collections of the Sunnī traditionist al-Nawawī (d. 676/1277). Around three-quarters of the *ḥadīth* in the two collections were identical but, because they were arranged in a different order, the two compilations conveyed distinct discourses.[12] This

9 See S. R. Burge, 'Compilation Criticism: Reading and Interpreting Ḥadīth Collections through the Prism of Fragmentation and Compilation', in *The Making of Religious Texts in Islam: The Fragment and the Whole*, edited by Asma Hilali and S. R. Burge (Berlin: Gerlach, 2019), 87–109, at 95–103.

10 See Norman Calder, '*Tafsīr* from al-Ṭabarī to Ibn Kathīr: Problems in the Descriptions of a Genre, Illustrated with Reference to the Story of Abraham', in *Approaches to the Study of the Qur'ān*, edited by G. R. Hawting and Abdul Kader A. Shareef (London: Routledge, 1993), 101–141.

11 See Newman, *The Formative Period of Twelver Shīʿism*, 193–201.

12 Louis Pouzet, *Hermeneutique de la tradition islamique: le commentaire des Arbaʿūn*

suggests that the *ḥadīth* in these two collections were not arranged in a random order but, rather, that they were very carefully constructed. This idea of intentionality in the construction and arrangement of *ḥadīth* collections (and smaller units of larger collections) also suggests that *ḥadīth* collections should be read and engaged with as they were created by their compilers: the arrangement of *ḥadīth* forms a discourse and a logical argument that develops as the individual *ḥadīth* are read consecutively.[13]

In another study of *ḥadith* compilation, Sylvia Akar argues that the important Sunnī *muḥaddith* al-Bukhārī was able to generate conceptual links between different chapters of his *Ṣaḥīḥ* by either citing the same *ḥadīth* in two or more chapters, or achieving a similar effect by using *ḥadīth* with similar *matan* in two or more chapters.[14] By doing so, Akar argues that the *Ṣaḥīḥ* creates a series of interlinked webs, where a reader makes connections with other chapters. Such a phenomenon suggests that *ḥadīth* compilers arranged the *ḥadīth* they had collected in a very considered way.[15] All of these studies of *ḥadīth* collection and compilation have shown that much can be learned from a close reading of a *ḥadīth* collection or a smaller unit (i.e. a *kitāb* [book] or even a *bāb* [chapter]) within a larger work. The method of compilation criticism takes the pragmatic assumptions that a compiler thought about the construction of a collection, what views and ideas they wanted to convey, and how best to achieve that. This chapter will explore the structure and arrangement of al-Kulaynī's *Kitāb al-ṭahāra* from these pragmatic assumptions. The analysis of al-Kulaynī's *Kitāb al-ṭahāra* will now look at each of these smaller units in turn and, building on Robert Gleave's analysis of the chapters on *tayammum*, will seek to understand the way in which al-Kulaynī structured the *akhbār* within the *Kitāb al-ṭahāra* to see whether the structure sets out a particular kerygmatic message.

al-Nawawwīya de Muḥyī al-Dīn Yaḥyā al-Nawawī (m. 676/1277): introduction, texte de arabe, traduction, notes et index du vocabulaire (Beirut: Dār al-Machreq and Librarie Orientale, 1982).

13 See also S. R. Burge, 'Myth, Meaning and the Order of Words: Reading *Ḥadīth* Collections with Northrop Frye and the Development of Compilation Criticism', *Islam and Christian-Muslim Relations* 27 (2016): 213–228.

14 Sylvia Akar, *But if You Desire God and his Messenger: The Concept of Choice in Ṣaḥīḥ al-Bukhārī* (Helsinki: Finnish Oriental Society, 2006), 75–76.

15 See also S. R. Burge, 'Reading between the Lines: The Compilation of *Ḥadīth* and the Authorial Voice', *Arabica* 58 (2011): 168–197.

1. An Overview of al-Kulaynī's *Kitāb al-ṭahāra*

Like many other books of law,[16] al-Kulaynī begins his *Furūʿ al-Kāfī* with a discussion of ritual purity. *Kitāb al-ṭahāra* is a significant work containing 340 *ḥadīth*s, spread over 46 separate chapters. As with many collections of *akhbār* that relate to legal issues, it is important that al-Kulaynī's *Kitāb al-ṭahāra* is not confused with a formal discussion of law – although the two genres often overlap in content, they are markedly different in what they are trying to achieve, as Gleave notes:

> The influence of the emerging *fiqh* tradition (both Sunnī and Shīʿī) can be detected in features such as the arrangement and presentation of *ḥadīth* compilations. Ḥadīth compilers, in turn, provided *fiqh* writers with a body of juristic material, which an accomplished *faqīh* could employ with acumen in his elaboration of the law.[17]

Whilst a collection such as the *al-Kāfī* can be an extremely valuable resource of *ḥadīth* and *akhbār* for legal discussions, it is not the same as a work of *fiqh*. At the same time, it is important to emphasize that that does not mean that *ḥadīth* compilers such as al-Kulaynī arranged their *ḥadīth* randomly but, rather, they can be seen to have arranged them in a specific order to convey particular ideas, engaging with the issue and topic at hand, which can often be legal in nature.

The 46 *abwāb* (chapters) of al-Kulaynī's *Kitāb al-ṭahāra* can be divided into five larger, discrete units or sections, each with a specific area of discussion. In some collections of *ḥadīth* the division of a large *kitāb* into more manageable groups of chapters can be hard to determine, and is often subject to a reader's interpretation, but in *Kitāb al-ṭahāra* the larger groups of chapters are clearly delineated, with each section being tightly focused on a specific issue.[18]

---

16 See Gleave, 'Between *ḥadīth* and *fiqh*', 352; Wael B. Hallaq, *Sharia: Theory, Practice, Transformations* (Cambridge: Cambridge University Press, 2009), 225 and 551–55; see also S. R. Burge, 'Compilation Criticism: Exploring Overarching Structures in the "Six Books"', in *Beyond Authenticity: Towards Alternative Approaches of Ḥadīth Narrations and Collections*, ed. Mohammad Gharaibeh (Leiden: Brill, forthcoming).

17 See Gleave, 'Between *ḥadīth* and *fiqh*', 350; see also Burge, 'Reading between the Lines', 196–97.

18 See the Appendix for a full list of titles of individual chapters in *Kitāb al-ṭahāra*.

	Theme	Chapters	No. of *ḥadīths*
A	The Water of Purification	1–14	108
B	Minor Ablutions (*wuḍū'*)	15–25	82
C	Major Ablutions (*ghusl*)	26–39	104
D	Dry Ablutions (*tayammum*)	40–45	29
E	Miscellaneous	46	17

This is a standard structure for a collection of *ḥadīth* and *akhbār* on *ṭahāra* and can be seen in both Sunnī and Shīʿī collections, such as al-Nasā'ī's (d. 303/915) *al-Mujtabā* (also known as the *Sunan*) or Ibn Māja's (d. 273/887) *Sunan*.[19]

2. The Water of Purification

The first section of *Kitāb al-ṭahāra* focuses on water used for ritual purification. This runs from Chapters 1–14 and includes 108 *ḥadīth* (nr. 3783–3881).[20] In general, these chapters discuss what can cause water used for ritual purification to become polluted. This is an important question since polluted water would make any ritual purification with that water itself invalid. The opening chapter, 'the cleansing quality of water', begins with a famous Prophetic *ḥadīth* stating that: 'water cleanses but is not able to be cleaned itself.'[21] This is followed by *akhbār* stating that water is always presumed to be clean, unless there is something obvious to indicate that it has been polluted.[22] This pragmatic presumption highlights two essential ideas within Muslim discussions on ritual purity: (i) the centrality of intention (*niyya*) in the performance of ritual action; and (ii) the primacy of reason (i.e. *ʿaql*), which is something that al-Kulaynī often emphasizes in his legal and theological thought.[23] Robert Gleave explains the

19 al-Nasā'ī, *al-Mujtabā*; *Sunan al-Nasā'ī*, in *Jamʿ jawāmiʿ al-aḥādīth wa-l-asānīd wa-maknaz al-ṣiḥāḥ wa-l-sunan wa-l-masānīd* (Vaduz: Jamʿīyat al-Maknaz al-Islāmī, 2000), 7:1–51; or Ibn Māja, *Sunan*; in *Jamʿ jawāmiʿ al-aḥādīth wa-l-asānīd wa-maknaz al-ṣiḥāḥ wa-l-sunan wa-l-masānīd* (Vaduz: Jamʿīyat al-Maknaz al-Islāmī, 2000), 8:44–118.

20 al-Kulaynī (tr. Muhammad Sarwar), *al-Kāfī* (Second Edition) (New York: The Islamic Seminary, 2015), 3:1–65.

21 Ibid., §1:1, p. 1 (nr. 3783).

22 Ibid., §1:2-3, p. 1 (nr. 3784–3785).

23 Newman, *The Formative Period of Twelver Shīʿism*, 101–3.

differences between cleaning one's fingernails out of a sense of hygiene and as part of a ritual: 'The first may be laudable, but does not form part of an act of worship (*ʿibāda*). The second is part of the means whereby a believer may perform his duty of prayer in a valid manner.'[24]

The rest of this section goes on to explain what things can and cannot pollute water intended to be used for ritual purification. This is done in a logical order, moving from obvious causes of pollution – often referred to as *najāsa ḥissiyya* (tangible impurity) – to those whose pollution is much less obvious, or even imperceptible – referred to as *najāsa maʿnawiyya* (abstract impurity).[25] Al-Kulaynī begins with the case of a dead body being found in a water source (§3), to a well into which someone may have fallen (§4), the potential pollution of a water source caused by a nearby cesspit (§5), then to the possibility of pollution being caused by unclean animals drinking the water (§6). This last chapter concerns what is termed *su'r* – the water that is left behind after someone or something drinks from it. In both Sunnī and Shīʿī theories of purity, if something impure, like a dog, drank some water out of a bucket, the water would become unsuitable for ritual purification. Ze'ev Maghen, who has written extensively on Sunnī purity laws, comments that: 'beasts deemed ritually impure (*najis*) by certain groups of *fuqahā'* are considered to impart a ceremonial deficiency to something beyond themselves (the water).'[26] Maghen uses the phrase 'ceremonial deficiency' to describe the state of the remaining water, as it is not necessarily considered to be unclean or polluting – so if someone drank it they would not become impure – but it is unsuitable for *wuḍū'* or *ghusl*. The same position is found in al-Kulaynī's *Kitāb al-ṭahāra*.

In several *akhbār* of Imām Jaʿfar (d. 148/765), it is clearly stated that the leftover water from drinking or from *wuḍū'* (*su'ūr* and *al-mā' al-musta'mal* respectively) of an unclean person is not allowed to be used for *wuḍū'*. In one *khabar* he says: 'it is permissible for you to drink the leftover water from which a woman during her *ḥayḍ* (menses) has drunk, but do not take *wuḍū'* with it.'[27] And in another Saʿīd al-ʿArāj asked the Imām whether the *su'ūr* from Jews and

24 Robert Gleave, *Inevitable Doubt: Two Theories of Shīʿī Jurisprudence* (Leiden: Brill, 2000), 17. For a detailed analysis of intent (*niyya*) in Sunnī law, see Paul R. Powers, *Intent in Islamic Law: Motive and Meaning in Medieval Sunnī Fiqh* (Leiden: Brill, 2006).

25 See EI3, s.v. 'Purity' (Ze'ev Maghen).

26 Ze'ev Maghen, 'Close Encounters: Some Preliminary Observations on the Transmission of Impurity in Early Sunnī Jurisprudence', *Islamic Law and Society* 6:3 (1999): 348–92, at 360.

27 al-Kulaynī (tr. Sarwar), *al-Kāfī*, §7:1, 3:8 (nr. 3826).

Christians can be used for *wuḍūʾ*, to which the Imām rules that it cannot.[28] This second *khabar* shows that the impurity of the non-believer can also be transferred to water. Based on Qurʾan 9:27, the impurity of unbelievers is a matter of concern in Shīʿī purity law.[29] This chapter gives details of a number of different types of people that contaminate ablution water or, to use Maghen's terminology, make water ceremonially deficient, namely: menstruating women (§7:1–4), Jews and Christians (§7:5–6), illegitimate children (§7:6), pagans (§7:6), those opposed to Islam (§7:6), and those opposed to the Imāms (§7:6).

Having dealt with the pollution generated by people outside the community, al-Kulaynī then moves on to potential pollution from Muslims themselves. In Chapter 8, the question is asked whether someone, on waking up in the morning, can pollute water by placing their finger in it before they have performed *wuḍūʾ*. The answer given is that the water is considered ceremonially deficient because someone cannot know if they have encountered an impure substance while asleep, which would then be transferred to the water.[30] In this case the issue is not whether the water is technically impure or not, that is whether it is actually 'ceremonially deficient', but its potential for being polluted.

Doubt over the ceremonial sufficiency of water can also be seen in the following chapter which discusses a very specific situation in which there are two drainpipes coming out of a building, one carrying rainwater and another urine, which then share a gutter.[31] If someone is splashed by liquid coming off the drain, do they need to perform *wuḍūʾ*? The answer given by Imām Jaʿfar is that if it is raining, i.e. if there is rainwater present, then ritual washing is not required, but it is required if it is clearly urine. In an earlier *khabar* we saw that water is usually presumed to be pure and ceremonially sufficient unless there is anything to substantiate its defi-

28 Ibid., §7:6, 3:8 (nr. 3831).

29 See Aaron Varricchio, 'The Purity of Non-Muslims in Shi'a Jurisprudence', *Journal of Shi'a Islamic Studies* 3 (2010): 617–184; for this issue in Sunnī thought, see Ze'ev Maghen, 'Strangers and Brothers: the Ritual Status of Unbelievers in Islamic Jurisprudence', *Medieval Encounters* 12 (2006): 173–223; Janina M. Safran, 'Rules of Purity and Confessional Boundaries: Maliki Debates about the Pollution of the Christian', *History of Religions* 42 (2003): 197–212; and Mahmoud Pargoo, 'Expansion and Contraction of Scripture: The Ritual (Im)purity of Unbelievers According to Shīʿa Jurisprudence', *Islam and Christian–Muslim Relations* 29 (2018): 215–239.

30 al-Kulaynī (tr. Sarwar), *al-Kāfī, Kitāb al-ṭahāra*, §8:1, 3:9–10 (nr. 3832).

31 Ibid., §9:1, 3:11 (nr. 3838).

ciency – in the case of the drainpipe: if there is rain, the liquid can be presumed to be rainwater; but if there is no rain, then it is clearly established as urine, which would necessitate *wuḍū'*.

The cases of the drainpipe and that of putting a hand in water before *wuḍū'* approach the issue of the 'unknown' in different ways. In the first example, an individual is consciously and knowingly placing his or her hand into the water, both choosing not to perform *wuḍū'* and not knowing whether their hand has come into contact with any impurities such as semen, urine or blood. The individual concerned is actively involved in creating a situation in which the water is potentially polluted and ceremonially deficient. In the second example, the individual is a passive actor and encounters the water without knowing the precise status of the water. In this case, the individual is required to come to a judgement about its status using what evidence is available, and in this case this revolves around the presence of rain: if it is raining, the status of the liquid is presumed to be clean; if it is not raining, the liquid can be assumed to be urine and polluting. The next three chapters (§11–13) lead on from this and discuss lavatories and washing afterwards. These three chapters relate what people should say and do in their everyday contact with a pollutant.

The final chapter in this section of the *Kitāb* returns to the specific theme of water for purification and deals with the amount of water that is required for ritual washing, both *wuḍū'* and *ghusl*. The main idea, conveyed in a number of *akhbār* with similar *matān* to the one given below, emphasizes the fact that only a little water is physically needed in order to perform *wuḍū'* or *ghusl*:

> Abu Ja'far, 'alayhi al-salām, said, '*Wuḍū'* is one of the boundaries Allah has established so that He finds out who obeys and does not obey Him. The believing people do not allow it (their body) to remain unclean. It is sufficient to use a small amount of water like rubbing oil on one's body.[32]

Most importantly, as will also be seen later, the ritual is seen as a means by which God can determine an individual's belief. The distinction between orthodoxic and orthopractic religious communities has been frequently challenged[33] and, here, the overlap between the performance of ritual and religious beliefs are

32 Ibid., §14:2, 3:19 (nr. 3883). [Some minor modifications to transliteration have been made]

33 Catherine Bell, *Ritual: Perspectives and Dimensions* (Oxford: Oxford University Press, 1997), 191–97.

clearly intertwined. In this *khabar* the performance of ritual is an outward demonstration of an inwardly held belief, the intentions behind which God alone can judge.

Al-Kulaynī's ordering and construction of these chapters concerning the water of purification reveal a taut and well-considered arrangement. Having established that water purifies, the chapters move through different types of events that an individual might encounter that would make the water 'ceremonially deficient' for ritual purification, moving from things that would clearly and obviously pollute the water to situations in which the purity of the water becomes much harder to discern. The chapter also proceeds from rare events to those that are encountered commonly, such as going to the toilet. These twin ideas shape the structure of this opening section of the *Kitāb al-ṭahāra*, ending with a restatement of the purificatory powers of water, which leads appropriately into the section on *wuḍū'*.

3. The Performance of *Wuḍū'*

The next section on *wuḍū'*, covering Chapters 15–25 and including 82 *ḥadīth*s (nr. 3891–3972), is focused on how to perform *wuḍū'* properly, with chapters giving details of things that can cause minor impurity (i.e. *ḥadath*). The section begins with something that is not specifically related to *wuḍū'* but which is seen as good practice, namely, brushing ones teeth in the morning. There are a number of *ḥadīth* in both Sunnī and Shī'ī sources that describe the importance of teeth cleaning.[34] This is not simply a concern of hygiene, but is also linked to personal eschatology: the noble watching scribes, who record individuals' deeds, are sometimes said to reside in the mouth, and good oral hygiene ensures that the angel who records one's good deeds is always present.[35] The noble watching scribes are not mentioned explicitly here, but the final *ḥadīth* in this chapter refers to the coming of an angel, and the need for a nice-smelling mouth:

> Abu 'Abd Allah, 'alayhi al-salām, said, 'When you wake up during the

34 Particularly the use of the *siwāk*; see V. Rispler-Chaim, 'The *Siwāk*: A Medieval Islamic Contribution to Dental Care', *Journal of the Royal Asiatic Society* 2 (1992): 13–20.

35 See. S. R. Burge, *Angels in Islam: Jalāl al-Dīn al-Suyūṭī's al-habā'ik fī akhār al-malā'ik* (London: Routledge, 2012), 170.

> night (for *ṣalāt* ([prayer]) you should brush your teeth; the angel comes and places his mouth over your mouth. Every word you say, he climbs with it to the heaven. Your mouth should have a pleasant smell.' [36]

This *khabar* clearly shows that there is a need for individuals to have pleasant breath.

Several chapters delineate the differences between Sunnī and Shī'ī ritual practice, with the Imāms stating that those who do not perform the ritual correctly invalidate their ritual purification and, consequently, also their ritual prayers. This is seen particularly strongly in Chapter 16 on washing, or not washing, the nostrils (e.g §16:3):

> Abu 'Abd Allah, 'alayhi al-salām, has said, 'You do not have to rinse your mouth and nostril (for *wuḍū'*); they are of the inside parts of the body.'[37]

Washing the nostrils (*istinshāq*) was a necessary part of Sunnī *ṭahāra*,[38] so the emphasis on not having to do this marks out specific Shī'ī practice. Shī'ī practice is also differentiated from Sunnī performances of *ṭahāra* in the way the face is wiped and how much water is used. In Sunnī practice, an individual: 'washes his face from forehead to chin and from ear to ear, and runs his moistened fingers through his beard, all three times';[39] whereas Imām Muḥammad al-Bāqir states that this is only done once.[40] This distinction between Sunnī and Shī'ī practice is most keenly felt in Chapters 19 and 20 which concern wiping the feet and dissimulation (*taqiyya*). This chapter raises the question of whether washing the feet (as opposed to wiping) is permitted if someone is performing dissimulation; the only two *akhbār* included in Chapter 20 read:

> I once asked Abu 'Abd Allah, 'alayhi al-salām, about the case of one suffering illness if it is permissible for him to wipe for *wuḍū'*. He (the

36 al-Kulaynī (tr. Sarwar), *al-Kāfī, Kitāb al-ṭahāra*, §15:7, p. 21 (nr. 3897).
37 Ibid., §16:3, 3:21 (nr. 3900).
38 EI3, s.v. 'Ablutions' (Ze'ev Maghen).
39 EI3, s.v. 'Ablutions' (Ze'ev Maghen).
40 al-Kulaynī (tr. Sarwar), *al-Kāfī, Kitāb al-ṭahāra*, §17:4, 3:22–23 (nr. 3904).

> Imām) said, 'No. it is not permissible.'
>
> I once asked him (the Imām), 'alayhi al-salām, about wiping for *wuḍū'* over one's shoes because of *taqiyya*h (fear). He (the Imām) said, 'I do not practice *taqiyya*h before anyone in three things: drinking intoxicating liquor; wiping for *wuḍū'*; and in mu'tah during the Hajj.' Zurarah said that he (the Imām) did not say, 'It is obligatory for you to disregard *taqiyyah* before anyone.'[41]

Imām Ja'far's response is very clear, stating that the feet must be wiped for the *wuḍū'* to be valid, both for those who are practicing dissimulation and those who are ill. However, in the previous chapter, a small concession is given in which the feet can be washed, but only after they have been wiped:

> He (the Imām) has said, 'If you take *wuḍū'* and instead of wiping your feet wash them, thinking that this is what is obligatory, it is not considered *wuḍū'*.' He (the Imām) then said, 'First you must wipe your feet. Then if you like to wash them and you did so thereafter wipe them to make it the last obligatory act (of *wuḍū'*).'[42]

The *khabar* that al-Kulaynī includes in his opening chapters on *wuḍū'* take his reader through the process of doing *wuḍū'*, but at the same time they highlight the differences between Sunnī and Shī'ī practices, and the need for those who follow the Imāms to perform the rituals correctly.

The chapters then turn to how *wuḍū'* should be performed when there are things that may present problems for its performance. Chapter 21 deals with performing *wuḍū'* with bandages; chapter 22 discusses what to do if *wuḍū'* is performed incorrectly; and chapter 23 gives a long list of what does and does not invalidate *wuḍū'*. The final two chapters deal with things that one might think would be a source of impurity (i.e. a *ḥadath*), but do not generate a need for ablutions: chapter 24 deals with stepping on animal excrement, which in most circumstances does not invalidate *wuḍū'*; and Chapter 25 deals with urethral discharge, other than urine or semen (i.e. prostatic fluid); again this also does not invalidate *wuḍū'*. As was seen in the final chapter of the first section, al-Kulaynī inserts a chapter that leads elegantly into the next section, and this

41 Ibid., §20:1–2, 3:29 (nr. 3932–3933).

42 Ibid., §19:8, 3:28 (nr. 3927).

is the case in this section too. Although chapter 25 deals with discharges from the penis that relate to *wuḍū'* rather than *ghusl*, the topic of urethral discharge leads into the discussion of *ghusl* seen in the following section.

As with the first section on the purity of water, it is evident that al-Kulaynī has given much thought to the way in which he has arranged the *akhbār* about *wuḍū'*. In Section A on the water of purification, al-Kulaynī first provides *akhbār* that establish how and why water purifies, after which there is a general movement in the structure of the section from impurities which clearly and obviously pollute water, to cases where the impurity is more difficult to establish. Section B on *wuḍū'* is very similar: al-Kulaynī establishes how to perform *wuḍū'* and then he outlines what invalidates it, beginning with those things that obviously invalidate *wuḍū'* to those that are more difficult to determine, and ending with things that one might think would invalidate *wuḍū'*, but do not.

4. Ritual Washing

The next section covers major ablutions, i.e. *ghusl*, and it runs from Chapters 26 to 39, covering 14 chapters and 104 *ḥadīths* (nr. 3973–4076). This section follows the general logic that al-Kulaynī has applied to the other sections that have already been discussed, in that he deals with topics in decreasing size of likelihood or applicability. However, as it will be seen, this section also deals with other related topics, creating a slightly more complex structure.

The first chapter in this section, Chapter 26, contains two *akhbār* which state when a major ablution is required. These are important since they establish the reasons for performing *ghusl*. This is especially important since in Shī'ī law there are significantly more events that require *ghusl* than in Sunnī legal thought. Al-Kulaynī's inclusion of these lists at the outset establishes the Shī'ī positions on those events that require ritual washing.[43] These two lists,[44] given on the authority of Imām Ja'far al-Ṣādiq, are not identical, but cover very similar ideas:

43 See EI2, s.v. '*Ghusl*' (G. H. Bousquet).

44 al-Kulaynī (tr. Sarwar), *al-Kāfī, Kitāb al-ṭahāra*, §26:1–2, 3:37 (nr. 3973–3974).

Reasons for Performing Ghusl	
§26:1	§26:2
after sexual intercourse	after sexual intercourse
Fridays	after menstruation
on the two Festivals	during irregular bleeding
on assuming *iḥrām*	a mother after childbirth
when entering Mecca	the child after childbirth
when entering Medina	a dead body
on the day of ʿArafa [9th Dhū l-Ḥijja]	before visiting the Kaʿba
on the day of visiting the Kaʿba to enter it	before entering the Kaʿba
19th, 21st and 23rd of Ramaḍān	when praying for rainfall
after touching a dead body	on the first night of Ramaḍān [preferable]
	on the 19th, 21st and 23rd nights of Ramaḍān
	on the 1st of Shawwāl [i.e. ʿĪd al-Fiṭr]
	on the 10th of Dhū 'l-Ḥijja [i.e. ʿĪd al-Aḍḥā]
	for *istikhāra*

The two lists are, unsurprisingly, largely similar, stating that ritual washing (*ghusl*) is required after sexual intercourse, on Fridays, in preparation for the two ʿĪds, when entering the holy areas, such as the Kaʿba, and so on. These cover performances of ritual washing which are a response to specific sources of pollution, such as blood and semen, but they also describe ritual washing made in preparation for deeper, more significant expressions of engagement with the Divine, such as entering the Sacred Precinct. The daily ritual prayers only require *wuḍūʾ*, but at specific moments of heightened sanctity and worship, such as Fridays, the two ʿĪds, during the rituals of the Hajj, or when entering into specifically sacred spaces, a major ablution (*ghusl*) is required.

As we have seen before, the chapters move through categories of people and events which require a major ablution in decreasing size, beginning with Chapter 28 which states that the Friday prayer: '[...] is obligatory on every male, female, slave or free'.[45] It then moves on to smaller groups of people: Chapter 29, whose title is ostensibly about the performance of *ghusl*, is actually concerned with *ghusl* after sexual intercourse – a smaller subset of people; whilst all people need to perform *ghusl* on a Friday, people who need to perform *ghusl* after intercourse at other times are a smaller group. The chapters then focus on issues of sexual intercourse: Chapter 30 deals with sexual intercourse during

45 Ibid., §27:1, 3:38 (nr. 3977).

which there is no ejaculation, Chapter 31 with wet dreams, and Chapter 32 with a situation in which a man, having performed *ghusl* after a wet dream, urinates and then discovers ejaculate. As in the other sections already encountered, these chapters deal with situations that become increasingly more remote from the main source of impurity, both the act of sexual intercourse and the polluting substance, semen, and also less likely to be encountered. This then moves onto discussions regarding what can and cannot be done while in a state of *janāba* in Chapter 33.

Al-Kulaynī then includes a series of chapters that discuss the implications of finding impurities on clothing. This was a common discussion in both Sunnī and Shīʿī law, known as *najāsat al-thawb*.[46] This begins with chapters that are directly related to sexual intercourse and *ghusl*, but then moves onto issues that are much more remote. The chapters discuss different types of bodily excreta that could appear on clothes, such as sweat from sexual intercourse, semen on clothes, urine on clothes, animal urine on clothes, blood and pus from wounds on clothes, and finally dogs touching clothes. Consequently, the chapters move away from sexual intercourse to other forms of *janāba*. Although al-Kulaynī moves into a broader consideration of impurity and ritual washing, these chapters are united by their focus on the physical act of washing. Physical washing, which also comes under the semantic field of *ghusl*, was often discussed in jurisprudence under the phrase *izālat al-najāsa* ('the removal of the pollutant'). For example,

> I once asked Abu 'Abd Allah, 'alayhi al-salām, about urine that pollutes one's body. He (the Imām) said, 'Pour water on it twice; it is water.' I then asked about urine, which pollutes one's clothes. He (the Imām) said, 'Wash it twice.' I then asked him about the urine of a child that pollutes one's clothes. He (the Imām) said, 'After pouring a small amount of water on it you must also wring it.'[47]

The general position found within the *akhbār* on the presence of pollutants on clothes is that the person wearing them is not required to perform either *wuḍūʾ* or *ghusl*, but the clothes need to be washed and cleaned, either the specific place of pollution, or the garment as a whole.[48]

46 Maghen, 'Close Encounters', 352; see also Wheeler, 'Touching the Penis in Islamic law'.

47 al-Kulaynī (tr. Sarwar), *al-Kāfī*, *Kitāb al-ṭahāra*, §36:1, 3:50 (nr. 4044).

48 Reinhart, 'Impurity/no danger', 9.

5. Dry Washing

The next section is on *tayammum* (dry washing),[49] and runs form Chapters 40–45. This section is much shorter and only contains 29 *akhbār* (nr. 4077–4105). Al-Kulaynī structures it in much the same way as the other sections. Gleave's reading of these chapters is that al-Kulaynī begins with the how to perform *wuḍū'*, after which he turns to more complex cases.[50] This is certainly the case: al-Kulaynī begins with *akhbār* that give reasons as to why someone may need to perform *tayammum* (Chapters 40–41) and when it can be used; for example, when an individual is on a journey and only has a limited amount of water (Chapter 42). The chapters dealing with more complex cases are then arranged in an order of decreasing applicability or likelihood of occurrence: being concerned about thirst (Chapter 42); only having ice or snow available after sexual intercourse (Chapter 43); using clay for *tayammum* (Chapter 44); and taking *tayammum* instead of *ghusl* because of certain health conditions (Chapter 45). This, again, suggests that al-Kulaynī had planned the arrangement of the chapters in line with this general scheme.

As has been seen in other chapters, the *akhbār* in this section also highlight differences with Sunnī legal positions. For example, al-Shāfiʿī argued that a search for water was a necessary step before opting to substitute the *ghusl* with *tayammum*: '*Tayammum* is never permitted except after the institution of a thorough search (*ṭalab shāmil*).'[51] Whilst this was the main position in Sunnī circles, Abū Ḥanīfa did not consider a search to be necessary;[52] which is also the position of Imām Jaʿfar al-Ṣādiq:

> I once said to Abu 'Abd Allah, 'alayhi al-salām, 'During a journey if I cannot find water when it is the time of *ṣalāt* (prayer), but it is said that water is nearby, must I then search in the right and left directions when it is time for *ṣalāt* (prayer)? He (the Imām) said, 'Do not search for water, instead take *tayammum*; I fear you may remain behind your

49 For a discussion of Shīʿī views on *tayammum*, see Gleave, 'Between *ḥadīth* and *fiqh*' and for a discussion of Sunnī views on *tayammum* see Ze'ev Maghen, 'Three Shāfiʿites in search of water: the indulgence of *tayammum* and its rigorous preconditions', *Der Islam* 82 (2005): 291–348.

50 Gleave, 'Between *ḥadīth* and *fiqh*', 356–57.

51 al-Shāfiʿī, *Kitāb al-umm*; translated in Maghen, 'Three Shāfiʿites in Search of Water', 306.

52 Maghen, 'Three Shāfiʿites in Search of Water', 307.

> companions and you may get lost or be eaten by animals.'[53]

Here, the performance of the prayers and keeping safe take precedence over the search for water. The position in this tradition and other *akhbār* in this chapter that water does not have to be sought in every situation, although found in Ḥanafī thought, was in stark contrast to the prevailing Sunnī positions. Although this section is small in size, it follows the general patterns seen in other sections of the *Kitāb al-ṭahāra*.

6. Miscellaneous *Hadīths* and *Akhbār*

The final section consists of only one chapter on 'Rare *ḥadīths* about *wuḍū*''. It contains 17 *akhbār* and is a mix of items, the underlying structure of which is hard to determine.

	Rare ḥadīths about wuḍū'	
E	Miscellaneous	
Chapter	No.	Title
46	1	*Wuḍū'* is the start of the *ṣalāt*
	2	*Wuḍū'* is the start of the *ṣalāt*
	3	Giving thanks for relieving oneself
	4	Not drying the hands after *wuḍū'*
	5	The cleansing of sin during *wuḍū'*
	6	Prayers said while performing *wuḍū'*
	7	The cleansing of sin during *wuḍū'*
	8	*Wuḍū'* is a part of faith
	9	The cleansing of sin during *wuḍū'*
	10	On purity after a menstrual period
	11	Wiping the back during *wuḍū'*
	12	Using rosewater for *wuḍū'*
	13	Touching bones that have been buried for over a year
	14	Falling asleep in a mosque and discovering menstrual blood or ejaculate
	15	Snake in a water butt

53 al-Kulaynī (tr. Sarwar), *al-Kāfī, Kitāb al-ṭahāra*, §41:6, 3:50 (nr. 4088).

16	Concerning what to do with blood from a nosebleed
17	Buying water at great cost

The first ten *akhbār* are linked by the theme of the theology of *wuḍū'*, as they discuss the relationship between *wuḍū'*, faith and the purification of sins. The two opening *akhbār* pair *wuḍū'* with the ritual prayers,

> The Messenger of Allah has said: *wuḍū'* is the opening of *ṣalāt* (prayer); takbīr marks the field of *ṣalāt* (prayer), and taslim marks the end of the field of *ṣalāt* (prayer).[54]

Another describes the efficacy of *wuḍū'* and which sins are washed away through doing it:

> Abu al-Hassan, Musa, 'alayhi al-salam, has said: 'If one takes *wuḍū'* for maghrib *ṣalāt* (prayer), this *wuḍū'* is expiation for the sins committed during the day that has just passed, except for major sins. If one takes *wuḍū'* for the morning *ṣalāt* (prayer), this *wuḍū'* is expiation for the sins committed during the night that has just passed, expect the major sins.'[55]

Both *akhbār* connect *wuḍū'* directly to the performance of the ritual prayers, as expected, but they say much more theologically. Firstly, ritual purity and prayer are inextricably linked and one cannot happen without the other: the ritual prayers are not valid without *wuḍū'*, and *wuḍū'* is always a preparation for the ritual prayers. This does not only mean that *wuḍū'* has to be performed in the correct way for the prayers to be valid, but *wuḍū'* is, theologically, the moment when an engagement with the Divine is being entered into and needs to be done with proper intent. Secondly, the *akhbār* that discusses which sins *wuḍū'* expiates emphasizes the personal eschatological danger of not performing the *ṣalāt*, and the eschatological profit in performing them: one's minor sins are forgotten when *wuḍū'* is performed, but only for the day; if the prayer is forgotten, one's sins will remain on an individual's eschatological 'account'.[56] This *khabar* also has a deeply negative eschatological impact on those Muslims

54 Ibid., §46:2, 3:62 (nr. 4107).

55 Ibid., §46:5, 3:62 (nr. 4110).

56 See Willem A. Bijlefeld, 'Eschatology: Some Muslim and Christian Data', *Islam and Christian Muslim Relations* 15 (2004): 35–54.

who do not follow the Imāms in the correct methods of purification: their sins remain and cannot be removed.

Of the remaining seven *akhbār*, the final *khabar* acts as a conclusion to the *Kitāb al-ṭahāra* as a whole, and the six before the end (§§11-16) return to the theme of water. However, there are some oddly placed *akhbār*. For example, one *khabar* discusses a snake entering and then leaving a water butt – why did al-Kulaynī place this *khabar* in this chapter, rather than in one of the earlier chapters that discuss animals and the water for purification? Why is the *khabar* about a nosebleed in this chapter? The *khabar* about someone falling asleep in the Sacred Precinct, or in the Prophet's mosque and discovering a source of *janāba* when they wake up, states that they must immediately perform *tayammum* before leaving the mosque, and then perform *ghusl*. This could easily have been placed in either the section on *tayammum* or the section on *ghusl* – and its inclusion here is unusual and unexpected. Although only tentative, these last few *akhbār* may reveal something about how al-Kulaynī is framing his discussions of the water of purification, *wuḍū'*, *ghusl* and *tayammum*.

On closer inspection, these six *akhbār* appear to have been hard to include in the other sections and chapters above, because they could have disrupted the main arguments that al-Kulaynī is making in each of the earlier sections. Consider, for example, the *khabar* about the rosewater and the snake in the water butt:

> I once asked Abu al- Ḥassan, 'alayhi al-salam, about a man who takes *wuḍū'* with rosewater for *ṣalāt* (prayer). He (the Imām) said: 'It is not harmful.'[57]
>
> I once asked him (the Imām), alayhi al-salām, about the case of a snake that enters in a hub (large water container) which has water in it and then comes out. He (the Imām) said, 'If one can find other water it should be spilled away.'[58]

In these two examples, the things being discussed are both perceptible and known: the snake was seen entering and leaving the water butt in the second example; and the rosewater is clearly rosewater. This means that these examples are discussions of tangible impurity and whether these two cases make

57 al-Kulaynī (tr. Sarwar), *al-Kāfī, Kitāb al-ṭahāra*, §46:12, 3:64 (nr. 4117).

58 Ibid., §46:15, 3:65 (nr. 4120).

the water ceremonially deficient. In the first example the use of rosewater is permitted because roses are not ontologically impure, and consequently do not impurify the water, meaning that the water continues to be ceremonially sufficient.[59] In the case of the snake, the snake enters the water butt and then leaves. This touches on a second issue that is found commonly in legal discussions on the water of purification, namely, the role of saliva (*su'r*) in making water ceremonially deficient. Ze'ev Maghen comments:

> [I]t is clear that saliva – unlike many other bodily fluids and secretions which are *najis* in themselves – essentially functions as a conductor or transmitter (or even extension) of the impurity of the creature whence it emerges. Indeed, saliva constitutes the most potent and most common transmitter of this sort in *ṭahāra* (as is also indicated by the extensive concentration in the works of *fiqh* on the problems associated with su'r).[60]

Snakes were not known to breathe underwater and were largely believed not to drink at all,[61] and so, although snakes were understood to be unclean, because they did not drink there is no possibility of the snake transmitting impurity into the water through saliva (*su'r*). These two *akhbār* could have been placed in the section on the purity of water, but they have the potential to disrupt and distract from the broader argument that al-Kualynī is making. These two cases, especially the snake, need more complex explanations and would seem to go against the other *akhbār* in the chapter, which state that only the water left behind from clean animals is ceremonially sufficient.[62] In the case of rosewater, the *akhbār* only discuss the presence of physical things within it (e.g. animal carcasses, bodies), or salt water; the addition of rosewater is neither of these. Furthermore, the *akhbār* which do discuss water with impurities are all focused on the quantity of water, and again the rosewater *khabar* does not fit in with the main point being made by the other *akhbār*; consequently, al-Kulaynī has included both of these in a general section of miscellaneous *ḥadīth*s to protect the clarity of his arguments in the chapters on *wuḍū'* and the purification of water.

59 Cf. Richard Gauvain, 'Ritual Rewards: A Consideration of Three Recent Approaches to Sunnī Purity Law', *Islamic Law and Society* 12 (2005): 333–93, at 342n30.

60 Maghen, 'Close Encounters', 360.

61 EI2, s.v. 'Ḥayya' (J. Ruska).

62 al-Kulaynī (tr. Sarwar), *al-Kāfī, Kitāb al-ṭahāra*, §6:1–7, 3:7–8 (nr. 3819–3825).

Two of the seven final *akhbār* discuss contact with things that one might think generate impurity, but do not: one discusses touching bones that have been buried for more than a year, and the other on blood from a nosebleed.

> I once asked Abu 'Abd Allah, 'alayhi al-salām, about touching the bones of a dead person. He (the Imām) said, 'If it is after one year, it is not harmful.'[63]
>
> I once asked Abu al-Ḥassan, 'alayhi al-salām, about the case of someone who had a nosebleed; then he blew his nose and parts of it became small segments which came into contact with his water container. Can he take *wūḍū'* with such water? He (the Imām) said, 'If nothing is visible in the water container, it is not harmful. However, if things show in it, he must not use it for *wūḍū'*.' I (the narrator) then asked him (the Imām) about a man who has a nosebleed while taking *wūḍū'* and a drop falls into his water container. Can he take *wūḍū'* with such water? He (the Imām) said, 'No, he cannot take *wūḍū'* with such water.'[64]

These two *akhbār* both refer to three types of potential sources of impurity: human bones, nasal mucus, and blood. The first two do not generate any concern, but the final case of someone with a nosebleed does raise issues.

As we have seen in the discussion of the chapter on *ghusl*, the Imāms are clear that a dead body requires *ghusl*:[65] human bodies are not believed to transmit impurity, but the act of dying was a source of impurity, which is why the deceased are required to be washed after death.[66] In Sunnī *fiqh* corpses were not perceived as being a source of impurity and did not require *ghusl*,[67] yet in one of the two *akhbār* seen above that gave lists of what events required *ghusl*, touching a dead body also requires a ritual wash.[68] This is in conflict with the Sunnī position. However, in the case of bones over a year old, there is no longer any source of impurity and the individual does not need to perform

63 Ibid., §46:13, 3:64 (nr. 4118).

64 Ibid., §46:16, 3:65 (nr. 4121).

65 Ibid., §26:2, 3:37 (nr. 3974).

66 See Leor Halevi, *Muhammad's Grave: Death Rites and the Making of Islamic Society* (New York: Columbia University Press, 2007), 68–73.

67 Halevi, *Muhammad's Grave*, 72; Maghen, 'Close Encounters', 385.

68 al-Kulaynī (tr. Sarwar), *al-Kāfī, Kitāb al-ṭahāra*, §26:1, 3:37 (nr. 3973); see also *Kitāb al-Janā'iz*, §31:1, 3:135 (nr. 4393).

a ritual washing (*ghusl*). However, this also seems to mark a difference with some Sunnī positions on bones, since there are *ḥadīth* that forbid performing *tayammum* in a cemetery as the dust cannot be separated from fragments of bone.[69] One reason why al-Kulaynī did not include this *khabar* in any of the chapters on *ghusl* may be because the theme of this *khabar* moves away from the strong emphasis on *ghusl* and matters relating to sexual intercourse: this *khabar* largely falls outside the parameters that al-Kulaynī set for chapters on *ghusl*. Similarly, the chapters on *ghusl* contain relatively little on menstruation or on the *ghusl* of a dead body, as these are covered in the following books.

In the case of nasal mucus, there is a general consensus in both Sunnī and Shīʿī legal thought that it is not impure and will not make any water ceremonially deficient.[70] Certain types of blood, though, can generate impurity and require *ghusl*. The types of fluid that generate impurity in both Sunnī and Shīʿī law are those that are associated with sexual intercourse.[71] Semen is obvious product, but vaginal discharge, menstrual blood,[72] and post-partum discharges (lochia)[73] are also conceptually linked to sexual intercourse, with some scholars arguing that they are rooted in the expulsion of Adam and Eve from paradise.[74] Nasal mucus is not associated with sexual intercourse and so it does not make the water used for *wuḍūʾ* ceremonially deficient. The chapters on *ghusl* are primarily concerned with what generates a need for a ritual bath, but also what to do when impure substances touch clothing. The discussion of cleaning clothes (*izālat al-najāsa*) was a common and specific debate in *fiqh*;[75] neither of these two *akhbār* relate to that discussion, nor do they relate to issues around sex and impurity. This would seem to suggest that al-Kulaynī wished to lay emphasis on sexual relations rather than on other forms of pollution such as touching dead bodies and menstruation in his section on *ghusl*. This is likely to be, in part, because he includes specific chapters on menstruation and the burial of

69 Katz, *Body of Text*, 254.

70 See Maghen, 'Close Encounters', 360.

71 See Wheeler, 'Touching the Penis in Islamic law', 99.

72 The regulations for a woman with irregular blooding was debated, see Haggai Mazuz, 'Revisiting Islamic Laws of Istiḥāḍa', *Journal of the Royal Asiatic Society* 30 (2020): 223–29.

73 See EI2, s.v. '*Ghusl*' (G. H. Bousquet); and Haggai Mazuz, 'Islamic Laws of Lochia', *Journal Asiatique* 303 (2015): 239–49.

74 Brannon Wheeler, *Mecca and Eden: Ritual, Relics and Territory in Islam* (Chicago: University of Chicago Press, 2006): 47–70.

75 Maghen, 'Close Encounters', 355.

the dead immediately after *Kitāb al-ṭahāra*. The extended discussion of *izālat al-najāsa* shows that al-Kulaynī is also engaging with common debates that were being held concerning purity at the time he put together his collection.

The last *khabar* to be discussed regards waking up in a mosque and discovering a source of pollution:

> Abu Jā'far, 'alayhi al-salām, said: 'If one sleeps in Masjid al-Haram or the Masjid of the Messenger of Allah and experiences a wet dream, one must take *tayammum* and must not pass through the masjid without *tayammum* until one is out of the masjid, then take *ghusl* (bath). This applies to one experiencing *ḥayḍ* (menses) also and she must take *tayammum* as mentioned. In the case of other masjids, passing through them in such conditions is permissible, but such people must not sit in the them with such conditions.'[76]

There are two important issues with this *khabar*. Firstly, this deals with the very specific case of falling asleep in the Sacred Precinct or in the Prophet's Mosque, and waking to discover a source of *janāba*, here a discharge of semen. Secondly, the ruling is different, and largely inconsequential in other mosques. In *fiqhī* literature there are often debates about passing through mosques while being in a state of impurity, known as *'ābir sabīl*, and we can see al-Kulaynī dealing with this in part here. It could be argued that this *khabar* could have been placed in the section on *tayammum*, but again, it does not fit there either, as the section on *tayammum* is concerned with situations where there is a lack of water; here, the issue is about waking in one of the two Holy Mosques, and what needs to be done in those very specific contexts. To include this *khabar* in the section on *tayammum* would have disrupted al-Kulaynī's focus on what to do when there is no water available in that section.

The final *khabar* in *Kitāb al-ṭahāra* restates the importance of *wuḍū'* and the water of purification.

> I once asked Abu al-Ḥassan, 'alayhi al-salām, about a man who needs to make *wuḍū'* for *ṣalāt* (prayer). However, he is not able to find water. He finds a certain amount of water which is enough for his *wuḍū'* but it costs one hundred dirham or one thousand dirham. If he has that much dirham to buy and make *wuḍū'*, should he buy the water or instead

76 al-Kulaynī (tr. Sarwar), *al-Kāfī*, *Kitāb al-ṭahāra*, §46:14, p. 65 (nr. 4119).

> perform *tayammum*? He (the Imām) said, 'No, he must buy. This kind of thing has happened to me and I bought water to take *wuḍū'*. What is bought (in this case) is a great deal.'[77]

This *khabar* returns to the theme of water and the importance of *wuḍū'* and with its discussion of purchasing water at great, if not extortionate, cost, it reveals the eschatological value of *wuḍū'*.[78] Importantly, al-Kulaynī gives his *Kitāb al-ṭahāra* a definite close and a fitting ending using a *khabar* that gives such importance to the performance of *wuḍū'*.

Conclusions

This analysis of al-Kulaynī's *Kitāb al-ṭahāra* has shown that it is organised in a coherent and ordered fashion. This can be seen in each of the sections, where the different chapters form a logical progression. In the section on the water of purification, the movement is from tangible to abstract sources of impurity. In the section on *wuḍū'* it follows the order of the ritual itself and so on. This shows that the work has been put together with care and consideration and, more importantly, that al-Kualynī is shaping the arrangement of the *akhbār* to convey ideas and opinions. Gleave compares al-Kulaynī's approach to later legal works that include more personal comment and analysis, concluding that:

> al-Kulaynī's contribution is masked by the technique of merely listing reports, whereas later authors did not suffer the same timidity in their investigations into the meaning of the Imām's words and deeds.[79]

For Gleave, al-Kulaynī's *al-Kāfī* marks an early stage in the development of Imāmī *fiqh*, which began with recourse to *akhbār*, before moving into more discursive debates. As Gleave shows, although al-Kulaynī's views may not be overtly expressed, as in a formal work of jurisprudence, he still manages to put across ideas through the way he shapes the material. This conclusion will highlight some of the more important beliefs and positions that al-Kulaynī is advocating or giving more prominence.

77 Ibid., §46:17, 3:65 (nr. 4122).
78 Maghen, 'Three Shāfi'ites in Search of Water', 312–13.
79 Gleave, 'Between *ḥadīth* and *fiqh*', 356.

One of the main aims of this chapter has been to understand the general principles of arrangement in *Kitāb al-ṭahāra*. Gleave typifies al-Kulaynī's approach in terms of establishing the ritual, before dealing with cases and situations which are more complex. Gleave also argues that al-Kulaynī's arrangement of the *akhbār* is structured according to implicit questions.[80] It is certainly the case that he begins his discussions by outlining the ritual, before dealing with more complex cases, but one common thread throughout the four main sections in the *Kitāb al-ṭahāra* (i.e. excluding the 'miscellaneous' section) is that al-Kulaynī progresses through the material from the most commonly encountered situations to those that are rarer or are experienced by fewer people. This may explain why al-Kulaynī includes *akhbār* about someone having sexual intercourse and only finding snow or ice to hand before the use of *tayammum* by those with a communicable disease. Whilst only finding ice after sexual intercourse is likely to have been a rare event, all adults can potentially be in that situation, however rare or unlikely it may be; but those who have a communicable disease are a smaller group of people. Understanding this general scheme of movement from frequent to infrequent may have an impact on how other chapters in al-Kulaynī's *al-Kāfī* are read and interpreted.

The arrangement of the *akhbār* seems to suggest an engagement with common debates about ritual purity that were circulating in the 3rd/9th century in both Sunnī and Shīʿī circles. This is something that Gleave notes in his analysis of the chapters on *tayammum*, and this slightly larger study corroborates these findings. Gleave comments:

> In short, the Imāmī jurists began to use *akhbār* in the manner Sunni jurists used *ḥadīth*; and their jurisprudence surely had an influence upon the collection and employment of Imāmī reports. The development of the Imāmī *fiqh* tradition, supported by the *akhbār*, rather than identical with them, enabled Shīʿī intellectuals to challenge the emerging (Sunni) legal orthodoxy on equal terms.[81]

In this way, it is possible to read al-Kulaynī's *al-Kāfī* as a means for Shīʿī scholars to articulate their legal positions within the context of the broader *Ṣaḥīḥ* movement that was happening at the same time. Unsurprisingly, throughout *Kitāb al-ṭahāra* al-Kulaynī uses the *akhbār* to advance Shīʿī positions on purity,

80 Ibid., 358.
81 Ibid., 382.

wuḍūʾ and *ghusl* and to engage in a quiet polemic against Sunnī jurists and their *ḥadīth* collections. For example, in the first chapter dealing with *ghusl*, he begins with two *akhbār* that detail the events that require *ghusl*, which are different to Sunnī legal positions. In contrast, the Sunnī *muḥaddith* al-Nasāʾī begins his general discussion of *ghusl* in his *al-Mujtabā* with a *ḥadīth* saying 'None of you should wash in standing water while being ritually impure (*junub*).'[82] This *ḥadīth* opens with a focus on orthopraxy, whereas al-Kulaynī outlines the Shīʿī position at the outset. In doing so, he is demarcating the Shīʿī space and conception of major ritual purity. The two *akhbār* that open the section *ghusl* also highlight the theological and spiritual aspect of ritual purity regulations in Islam by presenting ritual washing not simply as a response to encountering a pollutant, but as an engagement with the Divine in a variety of forms of worship, from the *ṣalāt* to the festivals of ʿĪd al-Fiṭr and ʿĪd al-Aḍḥā, to prayers for rain, and entering the sacred precinct. By no means is the opening of the chapter on *ghusl* the only place where he advocates distinctly Shīʿī views and a number of other examples have been noted in the discussions above; but in the opening of the section on *ghusl* the distinctive Shīʿī positions are stated particularly strongly.

Although al-Kulaynī's *al-Kāfī* is a Shīʿī collection of *akhbār*, it is important to take into consideration the fact that it was not written in a vacuum and he would have been aware of Sunnī positions on ritual purity, as well as some of the *ḥadīth* collections that were emerging at the same time in Sunnī circles. Andrew Newman has argued that the early Shīʿī *ḥadīth* collections provide a window on debates that were emerging between different Shīʿī scholars before and after the Occultation of the Imam;[83] in the *Kitāb al-ṭahāra*, it is possible to see al-Kulaynī arranging his material in 'dialogue' with the world around him, which also included Sunnī jurists. Gleave referred to the fact that al-Kulaynī's *akhbār* appear to be based on underlying implicit questions, and these questions frequently appear to be responding to Sunnī practices and articulating the Shīʿī response, arming Shīʿī scholars with the means to defend their practice among the Sunnī majority. While the text is not a direct polemic against Sunnī views of purity, the *ḥadīth*s he includes and the way he arranges them provides his Shīʿī audience with guidance in how to perform the rituals of *ṭahāra* in a dominant Sunnī context, but also with *akhbār* that testify that the Shīʿī rituals are the correct ones. Al-Kulaynī's *al-Kāfī* is a tightly

82 al-Nasāʾī, *al-Mujtabā*, 7:35.

83 Newman, *The Formative Period of Twelver Shīʿism*, 193–94.

considered compilation which, although not a work of *fiqh*, still manages to articulate and convey Shī'ī views of purity and ritual washing.

The theme of the community is one that dominates al-Kulaynī's *Kitāb al-ṭahāra*. The *akhbār* establish how the community performs the rituals, but also creates a deep sense of identity through ritual. A number of the *akhbār* in the collection separate and differentiate the Shī'ī community from outsiders: from Jews, Christians and Zoroastrians, but also from those who do not follow the Imāms. This is seen in those *ḥadīths* that deal with the uncleanness of non-Shī'īs, but also in the *ḥadīths* that deal with the performance of *wuḍū'* and *taqiyya*. This demarcation of the community can appear in unusual places; for example, in his discussion of water from bathhouses:

> Abu 'Abd Allah, 'alayhi al-salām, said, 'Do not take *ghusl* (bath) from a well in which water from bathhouses accumulate, because in it there is water which is used by one born out of wedlock and it does not become clean for seven generations. In it there is water used by one hostile to 'A'immah, 'alayhim al-salām. One who is hostile to 'A'immah, 'alayhim al-salām, is worse than the two others. Allah has not created a creature more evil than the dog but one hostile to 'A'immah is more worthless than a dog.' I then asked (the Imām) about the water of bathhouses from which one involved in sexual activities, children, Jews, Christians, and Zoroastrians take *ghusl* (bath). He (the Imām) said, 'It is like canals in which one part of water cleanses the other part.'[84]

This *ḥadīth* creates distance and space between Shī'īs and those who are not part of the community. Throughout al-Kulaynī's *Kitāb al-ṭahāra* ritual purity is not seen as something that separates Muslims from non-Muslims but creates and defines the Shī'ī community itself as distinct from those who do not follow the Imāms. As has been seen earlier in one *ḥadīth*, the ritual performance established by the Imāms is the means by which individuals are judged; those who do not follow the rituals established by the Imāms do not have their *ṣalāt* accepted by God.

This communal identity is not simply orthopractic but is rooted in spirituality and a sense of the Divine. Just as the acts of *wuḍū'* and *ghusl* turn the grubbiness of human existence – encounters with urine, excrement, and other bodily substances – and purifies them and makes them clean, many of the

84 al-Kulaynī (tr. Sarwar), *al-Kāfī, Kitāb al-ṭahāra*, §10:1, 3:12 (nr. 3846).

ḥadīths that al-Kulaynī included in his *Kitāb al-ṭahāra* move individuals from the mundane human realm into an engagement with the Divine. Al-Kulaynī fills his text with a deep sense of piety – *wuḍū'*, *ghusl* and *tayammum* are not simply about washing oneself of impurities; but rather, there is a much deeper, personal spiritual significance to *ṭahāra*. This is articulated most strongly in a *ḥadīth* towards the end of *Kitāb al-ṭahāra*:

> Once I visited Ali al-Rida, 'alayhi al-salām. There was a water jug in front of him and he was about to take *wuḍū'* for *ṣalāt* (prayer). I went closer to pour water to help him to take *wuḍū'*. He said, 'Hold it, O Hassan.' I then asked, 'Why do you stop me from pouring water so you take *wuḍū'* and I can receive reward for it?' He replied, 'You will receive reward, but I will be burdened.' I then asked, 'How can that happen?' He replied, 'Have you not heard the words of Allah, the Most Majestic, the Most Gracious, "Those who wish to meet (receive mercy from) their Lord should do good deeds and not allow anyone else to share in (their) worshipping their Lord." (Qur'an, 18:10) I am about to take *wuḍū'* for *ṣalāt* (prayer). I do not want anyone to share with me my act of worship.'[85]

This *ḥadīth* emphasizes the importance of piety and the fact that both *wuḍū'* and *ṣalāt* are a private engagement with the Divine, albeit one that is often performed in public and collectively. This emphasis on personal piety remains an important aspect of contemporary Shī'ī spirituality, and al-Kulaynī is able to articulate the way in which ritual and spirituality overlap.

Al-Kulaynī's *Kitāb al-ṭahāra* also provides a basis from which to approach a whole range of issues that people can face in the contemporary world. For example, in cases of palliative care, the use of a stoma is likely to cause a patient to come into contact with excrement, generating issues and concerns around ritual purity.[86] While al-Kulaynī cannot answer such questions directly, and although this is certainly not the place to explore the legal and ethical issues of a specific case like this, a number of *akhbār* included in the collection touch on issues of ill-health and can offer a means to negotiate complex contemporary issues. Above all, al-Kulaynī's emphasis throughout *Kitāb al-ṭahāra* on

85 Ibid., §46:1, 3:63–64 (nr. 4106).

86 Adnan A. Albar (et. al.), 'Improving Quality of Life for Muslim Patients requiring a stoma: A Critical review of theological and psychosocial issues', *Surgical Practice* 24 (2020): 29–36.

the importance of intention in the performance of ritual, but also the need for the use of reason (*ʿaql*) in the application of rules, provides an important base from which to begin to explore contemporary issues that involve concerns about ritual purity.

Above all, this chapter has shown that al-Kulaynī approached the arrangement of *akhbār* in a careful and considered manner. He appears to have applied underlying principles to the arrangement, moving from frequent and common situations to those that affect fewer people and that happen less often. Al-Kulaynī is also able to offer a critique of Sunnī ritual practices, providing the Imāmī community with evidence to defend their own ways of performing *ṭahāra* within a broader Sunnī context. While he includes many details that are focused on how to perform *ṭahāra*, there is an underlying spirituality that emphasizes ritual purity as an encounter with the Divine. Amidst all the grime of human life, believers encounter God through ritual and this encounter demands preparation and purification, making purity and ritual purification a central component in the experience of Shīʿī spirituality and worship.

Appendix

1. The Structure of al-Kulaynī's *Kitāb al-ṭahāra*

Chapter	No. of *ḥadīth*	Title
A	The Water of Purification	
1	5	The cleansing quality of water
2	8	The quantity of water that always remains clean
3	7	The case of a small quantity of water, water with a dead body in it, and the use of a man to wash his hands in it
4	12	The case of a well and things that may have fallen in it
5	4	A well near a cesspool
6	7	Taking water for *wuḍū'* from a well that an animal has drunk from
7	6	Taking water for *wuḍū'* from a well that (i) a woman has drunk from during her period, (ii) that someone who has had carnal relations has drunk from, (iii) that a Jew or Christian has drunk from, or (iv) someone who is an enemy of the Imāms.
8	6	Placing a hand in the water before the washing
9	8	Mixing rainwater with urine or clothes that have come into contact with urine
10	5	Water from bath houses and water heated by the sun
11	6	Places not desirable to use as a lavatory
12	17	What to say when going into and out of a lavatory
13	8	Draining urine, washing and if one finds no water
14	9	Quantity of water needed for *wuḍū'* and for showers
B	Minor Ablution (*wuḍū'*)	
15	7	Brushing teeth
16	3	Rinsing mouth and nostrils
17	9	Description of *wuḍū'*
18	10	Wiping the face and hands
19	12	Wiping hands and feet
20	2	Wiping over the shoes
21	4	Bandages and wounds

22	9	Doubts about completing *wuḍū'* or forgetting and doing things in the wrong order
23	17	Things that do and do not invalidate *wuḍū'*
24	5	Stepping over excrement
25	4	Fluid other than urine and semen
C	Major Ablution (*ghusl*)	
26	2	Kinds of ritual bathing (*ghusl*)
27	2	Matters covered by ritual bathing
28	7	Need for ritual washing on a Friday
29	17	Description of *ghusl*
30	8	Reasons for when ritual washing is necessary
31	7	Wet dreams
32	4	Finding fluid after a ritual washing
33	12	Actions after carnal relations
34	6	Sweating in clothes after carnal relations
35	6	Semen on clothes
36	8	Urine on clothes
37	10	Animal urine and faeces on clothes
38	9	Blood and pus on clothes
39	6	On dogs touching clothes or the body
D	Dry Washing (*Tayammum*)	
40	6	Description of *tayammum*
41	10	When *tayammum* is necessary
42	4	When you have water, but are concerned about thirst
43	3	*Tayammum* after sexual intercourse
44	1	Performing *tayammum* with clay
45	5	Performing *tayammum* because of a health condition
E	Miscellaneous	
46	17	Rare *ḥadīth* about *wuḍū'*

KRISTA M. RILEY

Online Narratives on Menstruation, Public Conversations, and Relationships with Religious Law

On 16 June 2011, Nahida Sultana Nisa, blogger at *The Fatal Feminist*, published a blog post entitled 'Important Announcement: I am on my period.' Continuing from the title, the post began:

> It's almost over actually, but someone tweeted today that her mother asked her, 'Are you wearing nail polish to announce to the world that you're menstruating?'
> To which I personally would have answered:
> F[***] yeah.[1]

The piece continued with a discussion on how much she loved menstruating, followed by two photographs of colourfully painted nails, and a note that she may do this every month.

The relationship of nail polish to menstruation baffled some of her readers, especially those who were not Muslim. It was only in the comment section of the blog post, in response to a baffled reader, that Nahida explained the connection:

> Muslims aren't supposed to wear nail polish because during ablution the water doesn't cleanse the surface of your nails ([nail polish] acts as a barrier) and the ablution is incomplete. But during our periods we're not required to pray, so a lot of us wear nail polish then.[2]

1 N. S. Nisa, 'Important Announcement: I am on my period', *The Fatal Feminist* (blog), 16 June 2011, http://thefatalfeminist.com/2011/06/16/important-announcement-i-am-on-my-period/.

2 This was shortly before the proliferation of water-permeable nail polish, which has created entirely new debates.

While Nahida did not ultimately follow through with her idea of posting pictures of her nail polish every month, she did continue to post nail polish pictures from time to time, each time with a clear reminder that this indicated that she was on her period. Of course, Nahida's monthly cycle as reflected by her nail polish would ordinarily be implicitly kept private from her blog readers, by the simple fact that readers did not normally see images of her hands, nor did she ever post pictures of her nails when they were not painted. Throughout her posts of nail polish pictures, it was clear that their function was not only to show off the bright and shiny colours she had chosen each month, but also to challenge the idea that menstruation was something to be kept quiet, to explicitly make public something that many would argue is best kept private.

The nail polish posts represent an adherence to a set of religious rules specific to bodies that menstruate, and practices coded as feminine (not performing the ritual prayer while menstruating and wearing nail polish but only when ablution is not required). At the same time, in a context where it could have been easily hidden – since her online readers didn't have any access to Nahida's physical appearance except for what she chose to show – Nahida's act of making visible her own cycle of menstruation, in direct response to norms that would ordinarily keep this hidden, also indicated a particular kind of challenge to certain structures of authority, and a mobilisation of the visual possibilities of the blog post toward that end. In telling and illustrating stories of menstruation, Nahida used her blog to rethink rulings and languages related to purity and gendered bodies within Islam.

This article will look at discussions about menstruation on three different Muslim feminist blogs based in the United States and Canada, including Nahida's blog *The Fatal Feminist*,[3] Kirstin Dane's *Wood Turtle*,[4] and *Freedom from the Forbidden*, written by a writer who uses the pseudonym Orbala.[5] Building on what Sa'diyya Shaikh has termed '*tafsir* through praxis',[6] and what Juliane Hammer has described as 'embodied *tafsir*',[7] I argue that blogs allow us to consider personal reflections and narratives of lived experiences that may be

3 https://thefatalfeminist.com

4 https://woodturtle.wordpress.com

5 https://orbala.net/

6 S. Shaikh, 'A Tafsir of Praxis: Gender, Marital Violence, and Resistance in a South African Muslim Community', in *Violence Against Women in Contemporary World Religions: Roots and Cures*, eds. D. Maguire and S. Shaikh (Ohio: The Pilgrim Press, 2007): 66–89.

7 J. Hammer, *American Muslim Women, Religious Authority, and Activism: More Than a Prayer* (Austin, TX: University of Texas Press, 2012).

left out of many genres of more formal theoretical or academic texts, allowing us to think about how people who menstruate develop and put into practice their own interpretations. Blogs present us with a window into how menstruation – among many other topics – is discussed in fruitful, creative, playful, and experimental ways. Moreover, many elements of the format of blogging – where posts can be published, and often are, as a kind of 'thinking out loud', without needing the green light from an external editor, and in spaces where bloggers and readers can easily respond to each other – lends itself particularly well to creative and experimental approaches to topics.

In looking at discussions of menstruation on these three blogs, I am interested in two main threads that interweave. First, I consider how the bloggers' public discussions of topics often designated as private (both within and outside of Muslim contexts) challenge many social expectations and, in doing so, provide alternate avenues for how these topics may be understood. Secondly, I look at the ways that the bloggers' online writing responds to dominant religious legal interpretations of these issues, emphasising the factors they point to that are often absent from religious rulings, which for their part are focused primarily on texts and on legal permissibility. I argue that, in this context, blogging represents not only an intervention into religious debates about gender and sexuality, among other issues, but also a reconfiguration of the terms of the debate itself, questioning where and with whom these conversations can happen, and what information and ideas are missing.

1. Visibility

At *The Fatal Feminist*, the nail polish posts were not the first time that the topic of menstruation appeared. In an earlier post titled 'menstruation and prayer', Nahida wrote about being told she should not be in a mosque while menstruating.[8] This post began with a detailed, even somewhat graphic, description of the beginning of her last period: waking up with a headache at 2:30am, noticing 'thin pools of blood' in the toilet, finding a pad, and later lying back in bed with painful cramps. After finally getting up and taking painkillers, Nahida headed to the mosque. In her post, she narrated the following exchange:

8 N. S. Nisa, 'menstruation and prayer', *The Fatal Feminist* (blog), 22 March 2011, http://thefatalfeminist.com/2011/03/22/menstruation-and-prayer/.

> In the prayer area, I sit while other women perform their prayers. One of them approaches me.
> "Why aren't you praying?"
> "Menstruating," I said simply.
> "Then you can't sit here."
> "Um. Why not?" I asked to be polite. In my head the reply was something like, *No, actually, I'm pretty sure I can.*
> "You're contaminated." I'm not kidding. She actually said this. "There are couches in the hall."
> "I'm pretty sure menstruating isn't contagious." I forced a laugh.
> "You'll ruin everyone else's prayers."
> "Really? Says who?"[9]

Nahida went on to talk about how the woman, whom she firmly believed to be incorrect, did not even seem to know where her point about ruining others' prayers came from.[10] She did not challenge the ruling that women do not have to pray on their periods, but expressed her exasperation at the ways that menstruating bodies come to be seen as dirty and contaminated.

A later post, written partly as a clarification after she introduced the nail polish series, elaborated on Nahida's understandings of Qur'anic- and *ḥadīth*-based rulings around menstruation, and made a strong argument that this notion of menstruation as a state of contamination had no basis in religious texts. She wrote with some frustration that her mother had been taught as a young woman that: '[…] once the menses were over she needed to clean everything she ever touched.'[11] Nahida contrasted this with a *ḥadīth* specifying

9 Ibid.

10 There is a difference of legal opinion regarding whether people who are menstruating can go into mosques; see, for example, C. A. Lizzio, 'Gendering Ritual: A Muslima's Reading of the Laws of Menstrual Preclusion', in *Muslima Theology: The Voices of Muslim Women Theologians*, eds. E. Mendeni, E. Aslan, and M. Hermansen (Frankfurt am Main: Peter Land Verlag, 2013): 167–179. Nonetheless, the legal explanations do not usually frame menstruating bodies as having the capacity to affect the validity of others' prayers.

11 N. S. Nisa, 'Menstruation in Islam (Quick Clarification on Last Post)', *The Fatal Feminist* (blog), 16 June 2011, http://thefatalfeminist.com/2011/06/16/menstruation-in-islam-quick-clarification-on-last-post/.

that if anyone gets menstrual blood on their clothing, all they need to do is wash the blood out with water, and then the clothing is once more appropriate for prayer. Commenting on the quoted *ḥadīth*, she wrote,

> Only the part that has blood, people! You don't need to run around lighting things on fire because you touched them. And even *this* doesn't imply that the blood is spiritual contamination – unless you want to force a patriarchal interpretation on it. Objectively all it says is that you should clean off the blood from your clothes, which–if you ask me–is freakin common sense. Yes, if your clothes are stained, do clean them by all means.[12]

The sarcastic and confrontational language, while not entirely out of place on Nahida's blog, suggests a level of indignation at the ways that, in her view, practical hygiene-related advice regarding menses came to position menstruating bodies as a 'contamination' that must be prevented from entering physical and discursive religious spaces.

In fact, Nahida identified this point about contamination as what drove her to start posting the nail polish pictures, discussed earlier. What she took issue with was not simply the idea that menstruating bodies should be hidden, but rather the discourses around the suggestion as to *why* such bodies should be hidden and the resulting implications for the spaces from which menstruating bodies are excluded. Posting the nail polish pictures – and describing the experience of menstruating in frank language – was both an act to make menstruation visible and a rejection of the idea that there was something gross or shameful about her body while it was in that state, something that could contaminate other bodies. The nail polish images then functioned as a way for Nahida to tell a different story about her body from the stories, language, and rulings that circulated around her.

On another blog, entitled *Wood Turtle*, writer Kirstin has also been quite explicit regarding her own narratives of menstruation. Kirstin has mentioned menstruation a few times on wood turtle, and the post where she discussed the topic in the most detail remains the most read and commented post on her blog.[13] Like Nahida, Kirstin wrote in detail about physical experiences of men-

12 Ibid.

13 K. S. Dane, 'Only women bleed: menstruation and prayer in Islam', *Wood Turtle* (blog),

struation. Although some commenters on the post objected to the detail of her narrative – one described it as 'obscene' – many also expressed gratitude for the open discussion of an issue that clearly resonates with them, echoing similar feedback received by Nahida.

Interestingly, a few years later, Kirstin also wrote about nail polish, wherein she referred to Nahida's posts, and shared a picture of her own nails.[14] The post also talked about starting a monthly nail polish series of her own, although she never followed up with this idea. As it happened, I had an interview with Kirstin scheduled not long after that post was published, to learn more about her experiences as a Muslim feminist blogger. When the conversation turned to the picture she had recently published of her nails, Kirstin explained to me that although she planned to post *pictures* of nail polish on a monthly basis, and only during her period, she did not actually follow the rule about not painting one's nails while menstruating. As such, it was entirely possible that her nails would be painted at other times of the month as well, even if she did not show it in pictures. As Kirstin explained to me, she was deliberately vague about this fact on the blog, so as not to lose certain readers whom she thought might judge her nail polish as '*ḥarām*' while not menstruating. Having people know that she had her period was seen as less likely to 'rock the boat' than a perhaps less strict approach to definitions of ritual purity (i.e. painting her nails even outside of her period). To put it another way, in this case, certain dominant ideas we at least publicly upheld (such as the need to avoid wearing nail polish to make ablution for prayer when not menstruating), in order for others (the notion that it is better not to speak too openly about one's period) to be subverted.

2. Qualifications

There are two important qualifications I want to raise in this discussion about challenging discourses of privacy around menstruation, lest we fall into the reductive image of the brave Muslim woman taking a stand against the backdrop of her oppressive Muslim community. First, let us talk about that back-

15 January 2011, http://woodturtle.wordpress.com/2011/01/15/only-women-bleed-menstruation-in-islam/.

14 K. S. Dane, 'Monday moments', *Wood Turtle* (blog), 9 December 2013, https://woodturtle.wordpress.com/2013/12/09/monday-moments-19/.

drop. Frank discussions about menstruation and sexuality in Muslim contexts are neither a recent development, nor unique to those located closer to the 'progressive' or 'feminist' side of the religious spectrum. In fact, it is rather ordinary to observe certain people not participating in communal prayer, or not fasting, and it is generally understood that phrases such as 'I'm not praying' are code for being on one's period. In other words, menstruation, and even the act of communicating to others that one is menstruating, is far from being an entirely taboo or hidden topic within Muslim communities, even if doing so more publicly may be frowned upon. Moreover, the idea of menstruation as taboo is certainly not unique to Muslim spaces and is also embedded in the social norms of the larger and mainly non-Muslim Western societies in which the bloggers live; consider, for example, the blue liquid long used in advertisements for menstrual products.

The second qualification on this topic is that the acknowledgement of the disruptive impact of one woman's openness around her body or sexuality can sometimes be taken as a corresponding criticism of women who are less open on similar topics, as if publicly discussing or acknowledging sexuality, bodies, and other supposedly taboo topics is always a sign of greater power or liberation. There is a danger, in that sense, of suggesting that certain bloggers' practices of writing in ways that explicitly expose or challenge these divisions of public and private are the only ways of demonstrating a kind of agency in self-representation. When it comes to discussions of Muslim women, this danger has echoes in imperialist rhetoric about the need to 'save' Muslim women through particular forms of sexual liberation – a rhetoric visible both in historical examples of forced unveiling under colonial powers[15] and in more recent examples of bans on various religious clothing in Europe and, more recently, Quebec. Jason Lim and Alexandra Fanghanel point out that: 'If ideas of sexual freedom and rights can resonate with colonialist discourses about "liberating" Muslim women from patriarchal oppression, then it may be that... the very appeal to sexual emancipation rests upon a Eurocentric vision of agency.'[16] In other words, seeing sexual openness or active challenging of norms around bodies and sexuality as inherently and uniquely liberating not only imposes new norms about how individuals should behave sexually but also feeds into

15 M. Yeğenoğlu, *Colonial Fantasies: Towards a feminist reading of Orientalism* (Cambridge: Cambridge University Press, 1998).

16 J. Lim and A. Fanghanel, 'Hijabs, Hoodies and Hotpants: Negotiating the "Slut" in SlutWalk', *Geoforum* 48 (2013): 208.

colonial projects regarding Muslim women. The openness with which Nahida and Kirstin talk about their periods should thus also be read in a context that does not accept this openness as the only way of claiming agency over one's body and the discourses that shape it.

This challenge is something that our third blogger, Orbala, has raised on her blog *Freedom from the Forbidden* about her discomfort in writing about provocative topics that she refers to broadly as 'sexy talk'.[17] While she explained in one blog post that she understood and rejected the basis for certain gendered ideas around modesty and appropriate feminine behaviour, she also described a lingering 'feeling of discomfort' when it came to certain topics, such as sex, sexuality, periods, and relationships.

In her discussion about who does and does not feel able to discuss 'sexy' topics in public, Orbala acknowledged the different risks and calculations that arise for different women, highlighting that the choice to write publicly has different consequences depending on each person's social location and sensibilities. In that sense, the problem of people not feeling safe or comfortable writing on such topics is a systemic one to be addressed at a systemic level, and not an individual limitation to be overcome. While she made it clear that she was in favour of people feeling comfortable and supported if they *want* to speak publicly about 'sexy' topics, she was clear that any judgement on an individual who prefers *not* to speak about such topics is unfair.

Even as Orbala proceeded in subsequent posts to write more openly about 'sexually provocative' topics, including menstruation, her points here raise an important concern about how the emphasis in this paper on public narratives of menstruation may be read. The graphic descriptions of menstruation raised through Nahida's and Kirstin's posts represent one important way that some Muslim feminist bloggers can challenge social expectations that would relegate menstruation strictly to a very private sphere, but this should not be seen as the only way for Muslim women (or anyone) to demonstrate freedom or empowerment as far as their bodies are concerned.

17 Orbala, 'The Privilege of Sexy Talk – and the expectation to remain faceless on Pashtun social media', *Freedom from the Forbidden* (blog), 19 March 2015, https://orbala.wordpress.com/2015/03/19/the-privilege-of-sexy-talk-and-the-expectation-to-remain-faceless-on-pashtun-social-media/.

3. Legality

Here I focus on the ways that questions about legal rulings on menstruation arise on the blogs. For this I return to Kristin's widely read blog post on the topic.[18] When I spoke to her about this post in an interview, she referred to the post's opening anecdote about her period starting again after two years of pregnancy and breastfeeding, and her sister-in-law's response that she could now enjoy a 'break'. Kirstin elaborated,

> I guess the idea behind the post is in the very first paragraph, where I'm like, oh wow, my period is back now, and oh, I guess I can stop praying? Why? Why do I have to stop praying, I've been praying nonstop for two years, [...] and then that's when I realised – well, why do we have to stop?

This questioning led her to reflect on what it means to take a 'break' from prayer, after not having done this for so long, and to look more broadly at discussions about Qur'an, *ḥadīth*, and jurisprudence (*fiqh*), as they relate to menstruation and prayer.

Much of Kirstin's post focused on challenging the ways this break from prayer during menstruation is conceptualised and explained in discussions she regularly encountered. If the 'break' from prayer during menstruation is seen as a mercy in response to the potential difficulties of praying while dealing with cramps and bleeding, she asked, then what makes menstruation different from situations of illness, where one might still be required to pray, even if the physical movements have to be modified? If it is a question of (menstrual) blood invalidating ritual purity, then how do we understand stories from Islamic history of the companions of the Prophet praying with nosebleeds and battle wounds, or, for that matter, the exceptions made for people with abnormally long menstrual flows, who are instructed to start praying again after a certain number of days have passed,[19] even when the fluid itself is identical to menstrual fluid? Kirstin also considered the implications of some of these ideas for how women and women's bodies are positioned within Muslim communities, often seen as impure or dirty, and denied access to certain spaces – and thus to particular forms of learning and worship – for a substantial proportion of their lives.

---

18 Dane, 'Only women bleed'.

19 See Lizzio, 'Gendering Ritual'.

Moreover, her comments in the same post about the value of prayer also highlighted why she saw the argument about menstruation being a time for a 'break' from being required to pray as unconvincing. Kirstin wrote that: 'prayer helps define what it means to be Muslim,' and that, 'It binds us together as a global community, provides solace, and expresses love for the divine.' In other words, being told she cannot pray while on her period was, for her, not an instance of being 'let off the hook' from a burdensome obligation, but rather one of being barred from an act of worship that was deeply meaningful to her, one in which she actively wanted to partake. There is a tension here between a religious practice that she believed to be (potentially) legally correct – that is, abstaining from prayer during one's period – and its ensuing detrimental spiritual impact.

In the same blog post, Kirstin also noted the implicit ways these principles get challenged: the women who seem to coincidentally get their periods only just after Eid prayer ends, or a woman she knows who would lie about her period in order to continue her Islamic calligraphy classes. While she was vague about her own position or practices, she wrote towards the end of the post that,

> If the injunction not to pray is indeed formed upon the common practice as taught by the Prophet, then it is unfair to argue otherwise. Women's bodies are routinely portrayed negatively in the materials aimed at educating us on what we can and cannot do. Even if the topic is dealt with respectfully and only notes the physical differences between men and women, relying on the traditional arguments still sets up unhealthy attitudes for women about their bodies.[20]

Her use of the conditional suggests that she was not fully convinced of the Prophetic source of this injunction, although she allowed for its possibility. In a note at the end of the post, where she explained the sources she used for Qur'anic translations, *ḥadīth*, and legal rulings in the post, she again wrote, '*I am not arguing against the injunction, but how it is presented in popular literature*'. In other words, she did not necessarily reject the mainstream legal (or *fiqhī*) position on menstruation, although she did not seem to argue in favour of it

20 Dane, 'Only women bleed'. Emphasis in original.

either. Nor did she reject the legal methodology that leads to the conclusion that people should not pray while on their periods; as she indicated, she would accept a Prophetic injunction as law.

She did, however, argue that regardless of the legal position one takes on some of these questions, there is more at stake than a reading of classical texts regarding the context in which one's prayers may or may not be valid. In other words, even if we accept the legal conclusions about when people can and cannot pray, we are left with questions about the implications of these conclusions for how people who menstruate come to think about their bodies more broadly. Moreover, she took issue with the additional justifications and rationales that were presented to her to try to convince her of the merit of the law (for example, that she should welcome the break), but instead had the impact of minimizing the difficulty and distance she felt as a result. Being told that she should be glad to have a break, for example, came as a cold comfort when that break was unwanted and a source of distress and disconnection, not to mention a contradiction with how she saw prayer discussed in most other contexts. Regardless of whether the break was indeed legally mandated, Kirstin's point was that it was experienced by her and many others as a hardship, and that the hardship needed to be acknowledged instead of being dismissed or explained away.

Some comments on Kirstin's post seemed to miss this nuance and focused on highlighting the clarity of existing legal rulings on menstruation. For example, one commenter quoted a *ḥadīth* along with Kirstin's observation that 'it is unfair to argue' against something that can be established as a command from the Prophet Muhammad, suggesting that, according to him, one does not pray on one's period, and the case is therefore closed. However, this supposed clarity was never exactly the issue. Kirstin did not negate the relevance of the question of legal correctness, but added to it that even the approaches understood to be legally sound often carry with them notions of certain bodies as inferior or dirty, notions that can have a real spiritual impact. In her words,

> The way in which this religious law is dealt with by many scholars, online literature, pamphlet Islam, multimedia lecture series, discussion forums and conferences, directly affects how women understand and relate to their bodies and is also used by men to help remove women from active worship and participation in the community.

Kirstin's writing on this issue leaves us with more questions than answers. What exactly do we do with this ambivalence? For religious practitioners for whom following the law is important, what happens when that same legal system seems to divide them from practices and communities that hold meaning for them? These questions point to an ongoing tension that the blog post leaves very explicitly unresolved.

At *The Fatal Feminist*, although Nahida's nail polish pictures represented a kind of adherence to certain rulings around ablutions and prayer, she also made it clear that she did not believe prayer to be forbidden during menstruation; instead, she merely said that she believed it is not required and acknowledged that some people do pray while on their periods.[21] Of the three bloggers, Orbala eventually came to talk most explicitly about her own practices related to menstruation and prayer, taking a position that went against dominant legal understandings much more overtly than either Nahida or Kirstin.[22] In contrast with Kirstin's implicit or ambiguous acceptance of the notion of not praying while on one's period, Orbala wrote that: 'I pray especially while I'm on my period; this is when I take my prayers most seriously.' Although Orbala did not directly explain this perspective, the suggestion from the rest of her comment was that her prayers took on additional meaning for her precisely in the moment when she was challenging the conventional ruling that the prayers have no legal weight at all. Instead, she infused that prayer with added importance that derived its value from somewhere other than legal validity or obligation.

So, what do we do, then, with the remaining ambivalence expressed both by Kirstin and Nahida? Kirstin's own readers expressed that they were unsatisfied by her lack of a solid legal position on the issues she explored; one reader commented that she was waiting for a 'punch line' that never came. And yet it is in this seemingly unsatisfying conclusion that I want to leave us, because in the lack of a 'punch line' is a suggestion that the 'punch' is located elsewhere. In other words, the bloggers, even in their engagement with some of the legal positions on menstruation, are conveying a set of priorities that do not lie only in legal re-readings. Instead, they challenge readers to consider the implications of legalistic discussions for the bodies such discourses govern. To connect

---

21 Nisa, 'Important Announcement'.

22 Orbala, 'Hypocritical Expectations of Women: how patriarchy devalues women's private parts – menstruation and public breastfeeding', *Freedom from the Forbidden* (blog), 28 March 2015, https://orbala.wordpress.com/2015/03/28/hypocritical-expectations-of-women-how-patriarchy-devalues-womens-private-parts-menstruation-and-public-breastfeeding/.

back to the earlier discussion about the bloggers' resistance to the exclusion of menstruating bodies from public spaces, I want to highlight that this absence of menstruating bodies from public discussions – perhaps aside from being objects of legal regulation – clearly has an impact on the outcomes of those discussions, and on how those outcomes can be experienced by the people most directly affected.

Conclusion

When I interviewed Orbala for my larger project looking at Muslim feminist blogs, she expressed surprise at the readers who reached out to her for religious advice, almost to the point of asking her for a *fatwa*, despite her lack of formal qualifications to issue one. Kirstin also commented in an interview on how many people, especially women, reached out to her for religious advice on issues such as *ḥijāb* and prayer, from places as far away as India and Zanzibar. She noted that such questions were coming to her, 'a woman in Toronto with two kids', and not, for example, 'a forum of male shaykhs'. In both cases, the scholarly authority that comes from formal instruction in religious texts and an expertise in interpretive methodologies seems less important that the accessibility of the writers, perhaps especially for women wanting to feel their questions are heard and understood. I am concluding with this point as a way of highlighting the resonance of writers like the three discussed in this paper. Blogging – and, we might add, newer forms of online and social media popular today – becomes an accessible way not only for them to express their viewpoints, but also for others to connect to them and feel heard. The comments left on all three of the blogs mentioned in this paper indicate that these three writers are far from alone in the ideas they express, and that there is hunger among readers for the challenges they bring both to social norms and legal discourses. The bloggers' writing on their encounters with dominant legal rulings calls attention to the moments when a narrow focus on law does not account for the effective stigmatisation, exclusion, or disrupted relationships to ritual that can result. This act of sharing their own experiences leaves open some of the relevant legal questions while calling attention to the effects of these discussion on bodies that menstruate that go beyond the regulation of ritual practice as it relates to purity. As we can see from the response to the posts, these challenges are widely felt and need to be taken seriously.

ALI FANAEI

Religious Purity and Impurity From Different Perspectives[1]

In many religious traditions such as Islam, Judaism and Christianity, phrases such as purity, impurity, cleanliness and uncleanliness and their derivatives form a significant part of the religious discourse.[2] Arabic phrases such as *ṭāhir, najis, ṭayyib, khabīth, qadhir, rujz* and *rijs* and their synonyms are found in primary Islamic sources (Qur'an and *ḥadīth*s) with high frequency. In Islamic culture, defining these terms, providing a list of their extensions, and identifying Muslims' duties regarding what is ritually pure and impure, is one of the tasks of jurisprudence (*fiqh*) and the jurists (*fuqahā'*),[3] although some mystics, philosophers, and moralists have also dealt with these concepts from mystical, philosophical and moral points of view.[4] Jurisprudential literature regarding ritual purity and impurity is comprehensive, rich and systematic, but discussions about these concepts from the jurisprudential point of view are mostly

---

1 I would like to thank Professor Muhammad Legenhausen for kindly editing the manuscript and for his insightful comments and suggestions. I am also grateful to my colleagues Dr. Wahid Amin and Mohammad Reza Tajri for their patience and encouragement, and my colleague Riaz Walji and my student Dr. Seyyed Rasul Mousavi for their invaluable assistance in finding literature references. Finally, I would like to thank my colleagues at Al-Mahdi Institute for organising the workshop in which an early draft of this paper was presented and for their efforts in getting this manuscript to publication.

2 See, for example, al-Ḥurr al-ʿĀmilī, *Tafṣīl wasā'il al-shīʿa ilā taḥṣīl masā'il al-sharʿiyya* (Qum: Mu'assasat Āl al-Bayt, 1416/1995), vols. 1–3; H. Maccoby, *Ritual and Morality: The Ritual Purity System and its Place in Judaism* (Cambridge: Cambridge University Press, 2009); B. J. Schwartz et al. (eds.) *Perspectives on Purity and Purification in the Bible* (Bloomsbury: Bloomsbury Publishing USA, 2008); and S.E. Balentine (ed.) *The Oxford Handbook of Ritual and Worship in the Hebrew Bible* (Oxford: Oxford University Press, 2020).

3 See, for example, Muḥammad Ḥasan Najafī, *Jawāhir al-kalām fī sharḥ Sharā'iʿ al-islām* (Beirut: Dār Iḥyā' al-Turāth al-ʿArabī, 1404/1983), vols. 1–6.

4 Abū Ḥāmid al-Ghazālī, *Iḥyā' ʿulūm al-dīn* (Beirut: Dār Ibn Ḥazm, 2005), 148–171; Muḥsin Fayḍ Kāshānī, *Mafātīḥ al-sharā'iʿ* (Qum: Kitābkhānah-yi Āyatollāh Marʿashī Najafī), 1:280–336; Ṣadr al-Dīn Qūnawī, *Sharḥ al-arbaʿīn ḥadīthan*, ed. H Kâmil Yılmaz (Qum: Intishārāt-i Bīdār, 1372/1993), 5–21; Ṣadr al-Dīn Shīrāzī, *Sharḥ Uṣūl al-Kāfī* (Tehran: Ministry of Culture, 1366/1987), 2:140.

focussed on material and bodily purity and impurity, whilst discussions from other points of view are scattered and marginal.

It has gradually become part of the religious identity of practicing Muslims that they observe their duties in this regard, and the religious discourse formed around ritual impurity has taken on an exaggerated identity role in Islamic societies and in political, legal and social settings with non-Muslims.[5] In modern times, in cases in which bodily impurity has been attributed to (a group of) non-Muslims as an intrinsic feature, this legal norm has created controversy for being incompatible with peaceful co-existence with non-Muslims, and their human and civil rights.[6] In addition, observing norms regarding impurity has created difficulties and tensions in different aspects of the personal and social lives of Muslims living in non-Muslim countries.[7]

This article aims to (1) look at purity and impurity from alternative perspectives such as mystical and moral viewpoints; and (2) show the impact that taking a particular perspective has upon the interpretation of the relevant religious texts and on the derivation of the relevant religious norms. In the first step, we must provide a philosophical analysis of the nature of purity and impurity in general. This analysis is the cornerstone of the 'metaphysics of purity and

5 Muḥammad Ḥasan Najafī, *Jawāhir al-kalām*, 6:41–89 and 21:227–322. For the development of Islamic ritual in general, see G. Hawting (ed.), *The Development of Islamic Ritual* (Routledge, 2017), and for the origin of Islamic laws governing ritual purification, see A. J. Wensinck, 'The Origin of the Muslim Laws of Ritual Purity', in *The Development of Islamic Ritual*, 75–93. See also D. Tsadik, 'The Legal Status of Religious Minorities: Imāmī Shī'ī Law and Iran's Constitutional Revolution', *Islamic Law and Society* (2003) 10 (3): 381–388.

6 Muḥammad Kāẓim Yazdī, *al-'Urwat al-wuthqā* (Qum: Daftar-i Intishārāt-i Islāmī, 1419/1998), 1: 138–141; Muḥammad Ḥasan Najafī, *Jawāhir al-kalām*, 6:41–89 and 6:41–44; L. Darwish, L. 'Defining the Boundaries of Sacred Space: Unbelievers, Purity, and the Masjid al-Haram in Shi'a Exegesis of Qur'an 9:282', *Journal of Shi'a Islamic Studies* 7, no. 3 (2014): 283–319; D. Tsadik, 'The Legal Status of Religious Minorities', 389–399; and Z. Maghen, 'Strangers and Brothers: The Ritual Status of Unbelievers in Islamic Jurisprudence', *Medieval Encounters* 12, no. 2 (2006): 179.

7 For the role of domestic religion in the lives of immigrant Muslims, see Shampa Mazumdar and Sanjoy Mazumdar, 'The Articulation of Religion in Domestic Space: Rituals in the Immigrant Muslim Home', *Journal of Ritual Studies* 18, no. 2 (2004): 74–85. See also the special issue of the Journal of Ritual Studies on 'Contesting Rituals: Islam and Practices of Identity-Making', *Journal of Ritual Studies* 18, no. 2; and D. Freidenreich, 'The Implications of Unbelief: Tracing the Emergence of Distinctively Shi'i Notions Regarding the Food and Impurity of Non-Muslims', *Islamic Law and Society* 18, no. 1 (2011): 54–5.

impurity'. The results that are logically derived from this analysis play a vital role in the 'epistemology and hermeneutics of purity and impurity'. In other words, the aim of this article is to provide a philosophical analysis of purity and impurity as two normative concepts and, based on this, to argue that the exclusively legal/jurisprudential approach towards these concepts has several objectionable consequences. Therefore, the right thing to do is to consider spiritual, moral, epistemic, and hermeneutical perspectives also.

Firstly, the jurisprudential viewpoint fosters ignorance of the symbolic meanings of the religious texts in which these concepts have been used, i.e., their implicit reference to spiritual, moral, and epistemic purity and impurity which are much more important than their legal indications. I will try to justify this claim by appealing to some Qur'anic verses. Showing that purity and impurity are not merely jurisprudential/legal concepts will render the relevant sections of religious texts more meaningful and the practices surrounding what is pure and impure more reasonable. Furthermore, if the religious way of life is to be differentiated from the secular one, their differences should not be reduced to their outer and legal aspects; rather, any difference in the outer and legal aspect of these two lifestyles should be a manifestation of deeper differences in their inner and spiritual aspects.

Secondly, in some cases, the jurisprudential approach leads to the misinterpretation of religious texts and results in the derivation of legal rules that may be subject to criticism.

1. The Nature of Purity and Impurity

In jurisprudential literature, discussions on purity and impurity usually begin by defining Arabic terms indicating these concepts. Muslim jurists try to justify their metaphysical claims regarding the nature of purity and impurity through such definitions. For example, the dispute over whether impurity is a real and objective property or merely a conventional and positive label stems from disagreement over the meaning of the relevant terms in religious texts.[8] 'Purity' and 'impurity' and their derivatives are amongst the normative terms in religious discourse. They are normative in the sense that alongside their descriptive meaning, they prescribe a course of action or inaction towards

8 N. Ṣāleḥi Najafābādi, 'Baḥthī Ijtihādī dar *Ṭahāra* va *Najāsa*', *Naqd va Nazar* 1 (1373/1994): 123–166.

what is pure or impure. For example, when we label something such as blood as impure from the religious point of view, this labelling means that contact with blood should be avoided, and what has come into contact with it should be cleaned, etc.[9]

Additionally, purity and impurity are thick normative concepts, meaning that unlike thin normative concepts, such as forbidden (*ḥarām*) and permissible (*ḥalāl*), their meaning is richer, and therefore they have the potential to form a discourse by becoming a central signifier for a network of concepts with intertwined connections.[10]

The first point to be aware of regarding the nature of purity and impurity is that they are either physical or non-physical properties. Physical purity and impurity have to do with our bodies and surrounding material objects in the natural world. From the religious point of view, physical objects are subsumed under two major normative categories: they are either pure or impure, and their purity or impurity is either essential/intrinsic or accidental/extrinsic. In Islamic culture, determining physical purity and impurity as well as deriving relevant norms of practice falls under the domain of jurisprudence.

While the jurisprudential discourse regarding physical purity and impurity is comprehensive and systematic, discussion of non-physical purity and impurity is scattered and incomprehensive. However, in primary sources, such as the Qur'an and *ḥadīth*s, one may find a wealth of raw material that can be used to develop and defend an interesting theory about non-physical purity and impurity. At any rate, non-physical purity and impurity can be divided into various types, including moral, spiritual, epistemic, and hermeneutical purity and impurity.

Second, to understand the nature of purity and impurity we need to look at the nature of normative concepts/properties in general. Metaphysically speaking, normative properties supervene[11] on some normative-making properties, and purity and impurity are not exceptions to this principle; they too supervene on some other properties of what is pure or impure. Let us call

9 al-ʿAllāma al-Ḥillī, *Tadhkirat al-fuqahāʾ* (Qum: Muʾassasat Āl al-Bayt, 1414/1993), 1:47–95.

10 For more on thick and thin evaluative/normative concepts, see P. Väyrynen, 'Thick Ethical Concepts', *The Stanford Encyclopedia of Philosophy* (2019); B. Williams, *Ethics and the Limits of Philosophy* (Cambridge, MA: Harvard University Press, 1985), 140–142, 150–152; and Kirchin, S. (ed.) *Thick concepts* (Oxford: OUP, 2013).

11 In philosophy, to supervene means: 'To be dependent on a set of facts or properties in such a way that change is possible only if change occurs in those facts or properties.' Online free dictionary, https://www.thefreedictionary.com/supervening.

these other properties basic properties, or pure-making and impure-making properties respectively. Furthermore, there must be a harmony in nature between supervening properties and the basic properties. Therefore, if the impurity in question is physical, the basic property on which it supervenes should be physical; and if it is non-physical, then the basic property should be non-physical.

To illustrate these points, imagine that there are two glasses of liquid on the table in front of you. You cannot arbitrarily call the left glass impure and the right one pure. They must differ from each other in having and lacking another property that makes the left glass impure and the right one pure. For example, the left glass might contain blood and the right one pomegranate juice. Similarly, we cannot describe the utterance of the same sentence by two different speakers as morally pure and impure, unless there is a further difference between them in having and lacking another property, such as the good and bad intention of the speaker, which makes the utterance of that sentence morally pure in one case, and morally impure in another.

In the context of discharging their religious duties, religious followers can identify what is pure or impure by knowing: (1) the relevant normative principles of their religion; and (2) the actualisation of the subject matter of these principles in a particular situation. For example, for Muslims to know that something is impure, they need to know as a matter of principle that blood is declared as impure in Islam and that what they have in front of them is blood.

However, in the context of norm-making, a wise norm-maker, whose decisions are not arbitrary or whimsical, needs a good reason to justify his decision in categorising things as pure or impure. Therefore, the question is: 'What is the justification behind religious normative principles of purity and impurity?' Putting it differently, the question is: 'What are the pure-making and impure-making properties of what is pure or impure?'

Regarding physical purity and impurity, one may find two different answers to this question in jurisprudential literature.[12] The first answer, which is the popular verdict, is that we do not know the reason behind the divine ritual laws. That is, the relationship between purity and impurity and what makes something pure or impure is conventional and positive, not real and natural. The jurisprudential argument for this position is based on the following two assumptions: (1) God as the divine lawgiver has used the terms 'pure' (*ṭāhir*)

12 N. Ṣāleḥi Najafābādi, 'Baḥthī Ijtihādī dar *Ṭahāra* va *Najāsa*', *Naqd va Nazar* 1 (1373/1994): 123–166.

and 'impure' (*najis*) and their synonyms with a new meaning in mind which is different from their ordinary meaning;[13] and (2) although God, as a wise norm-maker, always has good reasons for His legislation, in many cases His reasons are mysterious and unknown to us. All we know is that He has His own reasons for declaring something pure or impure, and we should trust Him in this regard.[14]

Based on these assumptions, religious principles declaring something as pure or impure are taken as positive and conventional, and thus our religious commitment requires us to follow them devotionally, without knowing the specific rationale behind them.[15]

The second answer is that 'purity' and 'impurity' have been used in the Qur'an and *ḥadīths* in their ordinary meaning.[16] This ordinary meaning refers to natural/real properties, supervening on other natural/real properties of what is pure or impure. Therefore, the relationship between purity and impurity and what makes something pure or impure is real, not conventional. Since we have epistemic access to these natural/real properties, one may conclude that, in the same way that ordinary impurity can be cleansed by ordinary methods and tools, so too can ritual impurities be cleansed by ordinary methods and tools.

An important hermeneutical implication of these two rival views has to do with the interpretation of the relevant parts of religious texts. The followers of the former view understand these texts as revealing the positive norms of religious law, whereas the followers of the latter view take these texts as revealing natural norms of religious law, i.e., a kind of law that can also be known by unaided human reason and experience. For example, while the first group argues that, according to textual evidence, something which is contaminated by blood can only be cleaned by water,[17] the second group would interpret these texts as prescribing just one method of purification which was available

13 By 'ordinary meaning' I mean the meaning a word has in everyday language before religion introduces a new technical meaning.

14 Muḥammad Riḍā Muẓaffar, *Uṣūl al-fiqh* (Qum: Mu'assasat Būstān-i Kitāb, 1387/2008), 247; and Yūsuf al-Baḥrānī, *al-Ḥadā'iq al-nāḍira fī aḥkām al-'itrat al-ṭāhira* (Qum: Mu'assasat al-Nashr al-Islāmī, 1363/1984), 1:401.

15 See, for example, Sayyid Abū l-Qāsim al-Khū'ī, *al-Tanqiḥ fī sharḥ al-'Urwat al-wuthqā* (Qum: Mu'assasat Iḥyā' al-Turāth al-Imām al-Khū'ī, 1430/2009), esp. 2:24–33.

16 N. Ṣāleḥi Najafābādi, 'Baḥthī Ijtihādī dar *Ṭahāra* va *Najāsa*', 124.

17 Zayd al-Dīn b. 'Alī al-'Āmilī (al-Shahīd al-Thānī), *al-Rawḍat al-bahīyya fī sharḥ al-Lum'at al-dimishqiyya* (Qum: Davari Publisher, 1410/1989), 1:305–308.

at the time of revelation, concluding that we may cleanse what is polluted by removing the pollution,[18] or by using disinfectant liquids or gels instead of water as they achieve the same purpose which is decontamination.[19]

My own position regarding the nature of religious purity and impurity is that they are real properties but are not necessarily physical. In fact, as I said before, the nature of purity and impurity depends on the nature of basic properties on which they supervene. If what makes something impure is a non-physical property, then the resulting impurity would be non-physical, and the method for its cleansing must be a non-physical process of purification. For example, it does not make sense to claim that my body becomes impure just because my mind is polluted by false religious beliefs. But it makes perfect sense to claim that my mind becomes impure if the false religious beliefs in my mind are the outcome of an irrational belief-forming process, for which I am responsible, and that to purify my mind from this epistemic impurity I need to replace my current belief-forming process with a more appropriate one.[20]

This metaphysical assumption about the nature of purity and impurity paves the way for the claim that purity and impurity are not just legal concepts that should be dealt with in jurisprudence. Rather, they have spiritual, moral, epistemic, and hermeneutical applications and extensions as well and, therefore, any jurisprudential investigation that denies or ignores the other applications of these concepts is vulnerable to the misinterpretation of the relevant parts of the Qur'an and Sunna. I will elaborate on some examples of this kind of misinterpretation later, but first we need to define other instances of purity and impurity and substantiate the claim of their existence.

2. Spiritual Purity and Impurity

Spiritual impurity is a kind of impurity that can occur in, and contaminate, the spiritual realm of human life. Monotheistic spirituality is a God-centric spirituality in which the primary purpose of life is to live with awareness of

18 Sayyid Sharīf Murtaḍā, *Masā'il al-nāṣiriyyāt* (Qum: Rābiṭa al-Thaqāfa wa-l-ʿAlaqāt al-Islāmiyya, 1417/1996), 105–6; Muḥammad Ḥasan Najafī, *Jawāhir al-kalām*, 1:317–18. See also Yūsuf al-Baḥrānī, *al-Ḥadā'iq al-nāḍira*, 1:399.

19 N. Ṣāleḥi Najafābādi, 'Baḥthī Ijtihādī dar *Ṭahāra* va *Najāsa*', 123–166.

20 For a similar position and argument, see N. Ṣāleḥi Najafābādi, *Pazhūhashī jadīd dar chand masa'alah-i fiqhī* (Tehran: Omīd-i Fardā, 1379/2000), 189–210.

God, and the ultimate purpose of life is reunion with Him. But because God is absolutely pure, in order to get closer to Him and finally achieve reunion with Him, we need to avoid what we may call 'spiritual impurity'. The prime example of this kind of impurity according to monotheistic religions is idolatry (*shirk*), which is the greatest sin in these religions. Also, every sin that one commits would be a source of spiritual impurity in the soul of the sinner because sinning is an instance of idol-worship in the inward sense of its meaning. Depending on the cause of the spiritual impurity, different techniques and processes are prescribed for cleansing and atonement.[21] If the sin is an injustice to God alone through violating His right, then sincere repentance would be sufficient. But, if it is an injustice to another creature by violating his or her rights, the sinner needs the forgiveness of the one who has been wronged as well.[22]

An interesting characteristic of religious spiritual impurity is that it cannot be taken as an autonomous category. Rather, it is a subcategory of moral impurity. In many verses of the Qur'an, God condemns polytheists, not just because they are polytheists, but because they do not have sufficient rational justification for their belief and practice. That is, they are condemned for violating norms of the ethics of belief and not discharging their moral duty in this regard. For example, in Qur'an 22:71 God says: 'They worship besides (or instead of) Allah things for which He has not sent any evidence, and of which they have no knowledge. The wrongdoers will have no helper.' In this context, wrongdoing (*ẓulm*) is a moral concept.

Verses like this imply that if someone makes a sincere effort in searching for the truth but ends up reaching the wrong conclusion due to elements beyond his control, not only is he not responsible and subject to condemnation and punishment, but actually deserves praise and reward. In other words, reaching true or false conclusions is not totally up to the researcher. What is up to him is his intention and endeavour, i.e., the process by which he reaches the conclusion. Therefore, an individual's state of spiritual purity or impurity depends on his or her intention and endeavour, i.e., on his or her moral integrity in the belief-forming process, not on the conclusion that he or she may reach by chance or luck.[23]

21 Muḥammad Mahdī Nārāqī, *Jāmiʿ al-saʿādāt* (Qum: Intishārāt-i Ismāʿīliyyān, 1386/2007), 2:236–7.

22 For a comprehensive discussion of different types of sin and the required type of atonement, see Muḥammad Mahdī Nārāqī, *Jāmiʿ al-saʿādāt*, 2:231–67.

23 For more on the ethics of belief, see A. Chignell, 'The Ethics of Belief', *The Stanford Encyclo-*

3. Epistemic and Hermeneutical Purity and Impurity

Epistemic and hermeneutical purity and impurity result from respecting or disrespecting moral considerations in the realm of cognition and interpretation. Here, the main idea is that there are virtues, vices, duties, and entitlements which are epistemic or hermeneutical in nature, but violating them counts as immoral behaviour as well. According to the Qur'an, epistemic and hermeneutical purity is a necessary condition for seeing reality as it is, for receiving divine guidance, and for the proper understanding of the holy books. In Qur'an 39:17–18 God says: 'So give good news to my servants, who listen eagerly to what is said and follow the best thereof. They are the ones whom Allah has guided, and it is they who possess wisdom.' Also, purity in general has an important epistemic and hermeneutical impact on the proper understanding of divine revelation, as it is mentioned in several verses of the Qur'an as well as in authentic traditions.[24] For example, in Qur'an 2:2 it is said that: 'This is the book, there is no doubt in it, a guidance for the God wary,' and in Qur'an 76:77–79 it is said that: 'This is indeed the noble Qur'an, in a guarded book, no one touches it except those who are purified.'

4. Moral Purity and Impurity

Moral impurity is a state of impurity acquired by intentionally and repeatedly committing what is morally wrong. Repeating immoral actions leads to the cultivation of immoral habits and vices and negatively transforms our character and personality. The scope of moral evaluation is comprehensive, covering all aspects of human life. There are five different realms which are subject to moral evaluations. These are as follows: (1) the realm of action; (2) the realm of speech; (3) the realm of feelings and emotions; (4) the realm of intention and will; and (5) the realm of beliefs and cognition.

---

pedia of Philosophy (2018). For a relevant discussion among Muslim Scholars, see al-Shaykh Murtaḍā al-Anṣārī, *Farā'id al-uṣūl* (Qum: Mu'assasat al-Nashr al-Islāmī, 1416/1995), 1:9.

24 For a similar discussion in the Christian tradition, see M. Westphal, 'Taking St. Paul Seriously: Sin as an Epistemological Category', in *Christian Philosophy*, edited by T. P. Flint (Notre Dame: University of Notre Dame Press, 1990), 200–26; and A. Munzinger, *Discerning the Spirits: Theological and Ethical Hermeneutics in Paul* (Cambridge: Cambridge University Press, 2007)).

We can talk about moral purity in all the above realms, and moral purification means cleansing all these realms from any kind of immorality. Moral impurity in the domain of actions is the result of doing what is unjust/immoral. However, according to the teachings of monotheistic religions, we can commit injustice against ourselves, and against God, in the same way as we can be unjust to another creature.[25] In fact, whenever we behave unjustly towards God or someone else, we have wronged ourselves as well.[26] Since justice makes sense only when there is a right to be respected or violated,[27] this means that the scope of rights in monotheistic religions is wider than what is normally recognised by secular worldviews. Therefore, idolatry is an instance of injustice,[28] and doing injustice to God is in fact nothing but doing injustice to oneself.[29]

Regarding the realm of speech, suffice to quote Qur'an 33:70 in which God says: 'O ye who have faith! Be wary of Allah and speak sound (well-founded) words.' Also, from the Qur'anic point of view, moral norms are applicable to the realm of feelings and emotions as well. An instance in which God refers to one of these norms is Qur'an 22:19: 'Indeed those who *like* indecency to spread among the faithful – there is a painful punishment for them in the world and the Hereafter'.[30] Furthermore, according to the Qur'an, the realm of intention and will is subject to moral evaluation and has enormous impact on human salvation. 'This is the adobe of the Hereafter, which we shall grant to those who do *not desire* to domineer on Earth nor to cause corruption, and the outcome will be in favour of the Godwary.'[31]

---

25 'And those who, when they commit an indecent act or *wrong themselves*, remember Allah, and plead [to Allah seeking His] forgiveness for their sins—and who forgives sins except Allāh?—and who knowingly do not persist in what [sins] they have committed.' (Qur'an 3:135, italics added); 'When Luqmān said to his son, as he advised him: "O my son! Do not ascribe any partners to Allah. Polytheism is indeed a great injustice."' (Qur'an 31:13).

26 'When you divorce women and they complete their term [of waiting], then either retain them honourably or release them honourably, and do not retain them maliciously in order that you may transgress; and whoever does that certainly wrongs himself.' (Qur'an 2:231); and 'We did not wrong them, but they themselves were wrongdoers.' (Qur'an, 43:76). For more elaboration on the definition of injustice and its different types, see al-Rāghib al-Iṣfahānī, *al-Mufradāt fī gharīb al-Qur'ān* (Beirut: Dar al-Ma'arifa, 2014), 315–16.

27 al-Sayyid Muḥammad Ḥusayn al-Ṭabāṭabā'ī, *al-Mizān fī tafsir al-Qur'ān* (Beirut: Mu'assasat al-A'lamī, 1390/1970), 1:371.

28 Qur'an 31:13.

29 Qur'an, 2:57.

30 Italics added.

31 Qur'an 28:83 (italics added).

Finally, regarding the realm of beliefs and cognition, there are many verses in the Qur'an in which God refers to our moral obligations about our belief-forming and belief-revision processes.[32] One of these verses is Qur'an 17:36 in which it is said: 'Do not pursue that of which you have no knowledge. Indeed, hearing, eyesight and the heart – all of these – are accountable.'

Conclusion

The above discussion clearly demonstrates that the meaning and application of 'purity' and 'impurity' and their synonyms in religious discourse should not be restricted to the physical realm and the domain of jurisprudence. By way of conclusion, I would like to highlight some of the hermeneutical implications of this assumption for Islamic jurisprudence (*fiqh*).

First, since 'purity' and 'impurity have multiple meanings and applications in different dimensions of human life, we need further evidence before interpreting a particular usage to mean physical purity or impurity and to establish a legal norm and obligation based on that.

Second, alongside their literal meaning, texts referring to physical purity and impurity have symbolic meanings.[33] Cleansing our bodies from physical impurity may have some impact on our physical health, but the purpose of religious obligations in this context is wider than this as it includes mental and spiritual health too. This wider purpose is to remind us that in the same way in which our bodies may become polluted and need to be cleansed and purified, the other realms of our existence can also become contaminated and need cleansing and purification. For example, when God says about the Qur'an that: 'No one touches it except those who are purified,'[34] we should not understand Him as just instructing us to clean our bodies and make minor ablution (*wuḍū'*) before touching the physical *muṣḥaf* of the Qur'an. This verse is also instructing us to cleanse our minds and hearts from spiritual, moral, epistemic, and hermeneutical impurities before reading, interpreting and contemplating the Holy Book; otherwise we would not be able to understand it properly and touch its spirit.

32 See, for example, Qur'an 2:111; 6:116; 6:139–140; 10:35–6; 10:68; 17:36; 49:6 and 53:27–8.

33 This point is emphasised in the history of Islam by thinkers in the Sufi tradition, such as Abū Ḥāmid al-Ghazālī in his *Iḥyā' 'ulūm al-dīn* and Sayyid Ḥaydar al-Āmulī in his *Asrār al-sharī'a wa-aṭwār al-ṭarīqa wa-anwār al-ḥaqīqa*, among many others.

34 Qur'an 56:79.

Third, considering the above discussion, some of the textual pieces of evidence from which jurists have derived legal principles concerning physical impurity should be understood differently. For example, when the Qur'an says: 'O ye who have faith! The polytheists are indeed unclean: so, let them not approach the Holy Mosque after this year',[35] it is referring to spiritual and mental impurity, as it does not make sense to claim that an unjustified belief would make the body physically impure. Their spiritual and mental impurity would pollute the spiritual atmosphere of the Holy Mosque and may therefore hinder the spiritual experience of the worshippers. There are several other verses which may be interpreted this way such as Qur'an 6:125 in which God says: 'Thus Allah lays impurity on those who do not have faith,' and Qur'an 10:100, in which He says: 'No soul may have faith except by Allah's permission, and He lays impurity on those who do not exercise their reason,' etc.

Fourth, in the same way physical impurity is sometimes the source of jurisprudential obligations,[36] spiritual, moral, epistemic, and hermeneutical impurities can be the source of spiritual, moral, epistemic, and hermeneutical obligations, respectively.[37] A verse in the Qur'an which elegantly summarises all these obligations is Qur'an 74:5 in which God addresses the Prophet: 'and keep away from all impurity!'

Finally, physical impurity cannot by itself impact our spiritual state of purity. For example, it is obvious that accidentally consuming impure (non-Halal) food does not pollute one's spirit. To have such an impact, consumption of impure food must be carried out in conjunction with an impure non-physical action, such as intending to deliberately disobey God's prohibitions. In the same way, the physical act of giving alms to the poor does not automatically elevate one's level of spiritual purity. For example, if your intention in almsgiving is to show others how generous you are or to embarrass the alms-receiver, then that intention will nullify any spiritual gains in purity, as illustrated by Qur'an 2:264: 'O you who have faith! Do not render your charities void by reproaches and affronts, like those who spend their wealth to be seen by people and have no faith in Allah and the Last Day.'

---

35 Qur'an 9:28.

36 Muḥammad Kāẓim Yazdī, *al-'Urwat al-wuthqā* (Qum: Islamic Publisher Office, 1419/1998), 1:170–188.

37 Two points: first, it seems that while spiritual and epistemic obligations are goal-oriented and therefore conditional, moral obligations are absolute; second, since spiritual and epistemic impurities are sub-categories of moral impurity, parallel to any spiritual and epistemic obligation we would have a corresponding moral obligation.

ARIF ABDUL HUSSAIN

The Existential Perspective on the Meaning and Implication of Impure Substances within Shī'ī Jurisprudential Discourse

The Sharia's designation of 'impurity' upon certain substances, together with the notion of 'physical purity', affects the lives of the faithful in a fundamental way.[1] Regulations on 'physical purity' (*ṭahāra*) and 'impure substances' (*najāsāt*; sing: *najasa*) inform the majority of Shī'ī Imāmī behaviours, from the accuracy of *ṣalāt* to interactions with non-Muslims, lifestyle and trade. The extensive Shī'ī jurisprudential discussions devoted to the proscription of trading with impure substances, and the issue of ensuring that both body and garments remain cleansed of impurities, provide insights into the Shī'ī Imāmī outlook towards impurities. For Shī'ī Imāmī individuals and communities residing in pluralistic societies of the contemporary world, wherein intimate interactions with the 'other' have become unavoidable, such norms curtailing the scope of societal and commercial engagement are problematic. In fact, the emphasis on the praxis of incessantly being vigilant, and staying clear of impure substances within the Shī'ī regulative system, has engendered the prevalent attitude among Shī'īs of the incompatibility of everything 'non-Muslim' with the life of a practicing Shī'ī Muslim. In view of this, some legists have speculated that the designation of impurity upon the 'non-Muslim' and 'wine', for instance, must be the outcome of historical misinterpretations of Sharia texts addressing them. If this is the case, then it is the distinctively Shī'ī-Muslim mindset of superiority over the 'other' that has negatively influenced their reading of texts pertaining to the ritual status of the non-Muslim; and, likewise, it is their mindset of disdain for intoxicants that has had the same effect with regards to the status of wine.[2] That having been said, the majority of legists subscribe

1 Ze'ev Maghen, 'Much Ado about *Wuḍū*'', *Der Islam* 76, no. 2 (1999): 206.

2 Having reviewed the status of non-Muslims in both Shī'a and Sunnī regulative systems, Tsadik concludes that, 'Shī'ī literature assigns Shī'īs an inherently superior status in relation to all other human beings, non-Imāmī Muslims included.' See Daniel Tsadik, 'The Legal Status of Religious Minorities: Imāmī Shī'ī Law and Iran's Constitutional Revolution', *Islamic Law and Society* 10, no. 3 (2003): 380.

to the impurity of both the non-Muslim and wine in addition to the impure statuses of the rest of substances conventionally understood as being impure.[3]

In light of the notions of 'form' and 'essence' as per the existential framework, this paper demonstrates that the proscription of trading with impure substances, and the strict protocols on being cleansed of impurities and maintaining a state of purity, was contextual to the way of life of the seventh-century Arabian community and their environment.[4] Firstly, it provides a brief overview of the elements of the existential framework relevant to this paper. Thereafter, it presents an etymological and conceptual analysis of the notions of the Arabic words *najis* (impure) and *najāsāt* (impure substances), their meanings in the Qur'an and *ḥadīth* literature, and the general context of pre-Islamic Arabia in terms of the prevalent attitude, norms and customs regarding cleanliness and hygiene. The next section of the paper focusses on one particular 'impure substance' in detail: the impurity of non-Muslims in Shī'ī jurisprudence. It outlines the evolution of the purity status of the non-Muslim, followed by an analysis of the relevant religious texts, jurisprudential arguments and justifications, and it closes with the perspective of the existential framework. Finally, the hermeneutic of 'form' and 'essence' is applied to the texts of the Qur'an and *ḥadīth* literature utilised by legists as Sharia evidences to designate other substances as 'impure' in a brief but critical survey.

The paper concludes that:

1. The designation of *najis* in relation to human beings merely signifies a state of spiritual or moral deficiency.
2. The impure nature of certain substances, such as wine, cannot be sourced accurately.
3. The substances warranting the designation of being 'impure' are in fact merely 'unhygienic' substances (*khabatha*). As such, their consumption or presence on the body is detrimental at a physical level, and incom-

3 The majority of Shī'ī Imāmī scholars believe all non-Muslims, which includes *ahl al-kitāb*, are 'impure' and 'polluting'. See Janina M. Safran, 'Rules of Purity and Confessional Boundaries: Maliki Debates about the Pollution of the Christian', *History of Religions* 42, no. 3 (2003): 201.

4 The existential framework is a legal methodology developed by the author. For more information, see 'The Conflict between the Actual and Apparent Regulations' – Part 2: The Solution of 'The Existential Framework' in the 'Academic Articles' section on the author's personal website: https://shaykharif.com/works.

patible with a sense of spirituality. However, their presence upon the body or garments does not impact the status of the obligatory prayer (*ṣalāt*) in essence.

4. The stringent proscription of trading with the Sharia-designated 'impure' substances was not due to their impurity per se; rather, it was the result of either the lack of any conventionally acceptable utility of such substances, or the broader notion of curtailing corruption of the individual and community, or both, as in the case of the proscription of selling wine during the revelatory era.

5. Essence and Form: Qu'ran and *Ḥadīths*

5.1 Form and Essence

When the existential theory of form and essence is applied to the domain of the Sharia, every regulation is deemed to be a form or formulation whose function is to promote a particular facet of growth in line with 'the existential property of growth'.[5] The growth facet of a regulation is its intended objective in light

5 The nature of existence is to be entified and dynamic (*al-ḥaraka al-jawhariyya*). It is a motion of perpetual 'growth' from a state of potentiality to a state of actuality in both the physical and conscious/mental aspects of things. Hence, 'growth' is a property of existence. An implication of this is that the status of the relations of things vis-à-vis human behaviour is also dynamic. In the mind of God, the status of the relation of a thing to human behaviour can be said to consist of three considerations: the thing's status in terms of its benefit and harm in relation to the human (known as 'the theoretical criterion of the regulation', *milāk al-ḥukm*, in *uṣūl al-fiqh*), the intention of God for that particular theoretical criterion to be a regulation (*irādat al-ḥukm* in *uṣūl al-fiqh*), and the formulation of the regulation in His mind (*i'tibār al-ḥukm* in *uṣūl al-fiqh*). Periodically, God has expressed these regulations to humanity via the Prophets (*ibrāz al-ḥukm* in *uṣūl al-fiqh*). There is a causal relationship between (a) existence, (b) the statuses of the relations of things vis-à-vis human behaviour in the mind of God, and (c) the Sharia regulations. The property of 'growth' in existence means that all its instantiations are in motion (or a state of change) which causes the statuses of the relations of things vis-à-vis human behaviour to change, which in turn causes regulations to change. Therefore, 'the existential property of growth' is the cause of all regulations. It necessitates change in regulations, and it is the 'end' or objective of all regulations. Hence, it is termed as 'the spirit of the regulation' (*rūḥ al-ḥukm*).

'The theoretical criterion (*al-milāk*) of a particular behaviour' and 'the intention (*al-irāda*) for its adoption' constitute the 'essence' or 'spirit' of the particular regulation, or 'the particular desired growth property of the regulation' (*al-rūḥ al-khāṣṣ*

of which it is formulated. The regulation is always formulated within and for a particular existential context; hence, its formulation is time- and space-bound, or contextual, and its intended objective, or essence, is universal.[6] At times, the objective becomes clear by studying the regulative formulation of a particular behaviour and its circumstances. For instance, the Sharia evidence from which is derived the regulative formulation of the necessity of having two female witnesses in place of a single male witness provides the rationale for the stipulation – which is that the second witness can serve as a reminder for the first should the latter forget.[7] This regulative formulation was pragmatically fashioned in and for a setting in which females were not generally accustomed to retaining information as compared to their male counterparts.[8] In view of this, it is possible to extrapolate the essence of this particular regulation, which is 'to ensure the accuracy of testimonials'. In turn, this essence (of 'ensuring the accuracy of testimonials'), and its contextually based regulative formula-

li-l-ḥukm). Whereas the linguistic formulation of a given regulation, which is derived from Sharia texts, is a particular 'form of the regulation' (*ṣūrat al-ḥukm*). The 'forms' of regulations are extensions (*maṣādīq*) of the desired 'essences' of the regulations. The idea of essence (*rūḥ*) is a distinctive feature of the existential framework setting it apart from the methodology prevalent in current *uṣūl al-fiqh* discourse. For while the latter focuses on the accuracy of the 'form' of the regulation (*ṣūrat al-ḥukm*) and hence is formalistic (*ṣūrī/ṣuwarī*), the existential framework is 'essence-based' (*rūḥī*). It focuses on what 'the forms' are conveying in terms of their particular growth properties, and it endeavours to secure those properties in the derivation of subsequent rulings in differing contexts. For more information, see 'The Conflict between the Actual and Apparent Regulations – Part 2: The Solution of The Existential Framework', in the 'Academic Articles' section on the author's personal website: https://shaykharif.com/works.

6 The expression 'existential context' refers to contexts in which the statuses of the relations of things vis-à-vis human behaviour is the same. The phenomenon of different existential contexts is the result of 'the existential property of growth', and they are 'different' to one another insofar as the statuses of the relations of things vis-à-vis human behaviour differ. The appropriateness of a regulative formulation to its particular existential context is measured in terms of its efficacy to facilitate the 'growth' of the individual and collective. The function of the legist, therefore, is to derive regulative forms that are 'most optimal' in facilitating the intellectual, moral and spiritual 'growth' of individuals and collectivities of all the different existential contexts. This is because regulative formulations pertaining to the existential contexts of the revelatory era will not be 'the most optimal' forms for the growth of individuals and collectivities of other existential contexts.

7 See Qur'an 2:282.

8 Leila Ahmed, *Women and Gender in Islam: Historical Roots of a Modern Debate* (New Haven & London: Yale University Press, 1992), 17 and 27–8.

tions, contribute to a more general facet of growth: the sound functioning of a just society.

At other times, the essence of a regulation is extrapolated by studying a variety of texts discussing the same subject in differing contexts. For instance, consider the regulation of the impurity of *ahl al-kitāb* (the people of the Book): there are traditions prohibiting the consumption of the food of Christians from their utensils;[9] then, there are other traditions stating that the Imāms had Christian maids.[10] Additionally, the Qur'an permits marriage with *ahl al-kitāb*.[11] When these Sharia evidences are analysed holistically, it is evident that the necessity of washing utensils was merely a means of ensuring that no trace of the detrimental substances of alcohol and pork remained upon them. It was not due to the 'physical' impurity of *ahl al-kitāb*, which is the majority view of Shīʿī Imāmī Scholars today.[12] Another way of determining the contextual, non-essential nature of a regulation is by ascertaining whether there are any exceptions to the general rule. For instance, the strict prerequisite of ensuring that the body and garments are cleansed from all traces of urine

9 See Muḥammad b. Yaʿqūb al-Kulaynī, *Furūʿ al-Kāfī*, in *Mawsūʿat al-kutub al-arbaʿa fī aḥādīth al-nabī wa-l-ʿitra*, ed. Muḥammad Jaʿfar Shams al-Dīn (Beirut: Dār al-Taʿāruf li-l-Maṭbūʿāt, 1998), 6:277–9. The reports are also quoted and discussed in Taqī al-Ṭabāṭabāʾī al-Qummī, *Mabānī minhāj al-ṣāliḥīn* (Beirut: Dār al-Surūr, 1997), 3:254–65.

10 See report no. 11 in al-Ḥurr al-ʿĀmilī, *Tafṣīl wasāʾil al-shīʿa* (Qum: Muʾassasat Āl al-Bayt li-Iḥyāʾ al-Turāth, 1990), 3:518–20. The report is also quoted in al-Ṭabāṭabāʾī, *Mabānī minhāj al-ṣāliḥīn*, 3:262.

11 See Qur'an 5:5.

12 As will be discussed, the majority of Shīʿī Imāmī scholars from the fifth/eleventh century onwards until the fourteenth/twentieth century have always posited the impurity of all non-Muslims. Despite some very notable twentieth-century scholars asserting the contrary, the foremost Shīʿī legists, namely Ayatollahs Khūʾī and Khumaynī whom the majority of the Shīʿī community considered as their 'sources of emulation' (*marjaʿ al-taqlīd*), maintained the traditional official position, even though their advanced classes in *fiqh* (*dars al-khārij*) and their elaborated *fiqhī* works (*al-fiqh al-istidlālī*) present arguments and justifications to the contrary, the essence of which is utilised in this paper. Some of the foremost Shīʿī legists of the twenty-first century have declared the purity of *ahl al-kitāb* (but not other non-Muslims), such as Ayatollah Sīstanī. (See https//Sistani.org.) However, it may be regarded by objective onlookers as a token gesture because the other regulations associated with 'the impurity of non-Muslims' still apply to *ahl al-kitāb*. Hence, in this paper the phrase 'the majority of Shīʿī scholars' (and its like) vis-à-vis the assertion of the impurity of non-Muslims refers specifically to Shīʿī Imāmī scholars from the fifth/eleventh century onwards until the fourteenth/twentieth century; however, it is still an apt expression for today.

prior to the *ṣalāt* is relaxed at the time of washing the urinary organ when the possibility of drops of urine, or water mixed with urine, splashing upon the body or clothes is significant.[13]

5.2 Methodological Considerations of the Existential Framework Pertinent to this Paper

In terms of Sharia evidences, the Qur'an is designated as 'the heavier weight' in comparison with *ahl al-bayt* – which is the other 'heavy weight' – in the famous report attributed to the Prophet.[14] This, together with the cardinal rules of: (a) the contingency of the validity of *ḥadīth*s (reports of either the Prophet or Imāms) upon their not contradicting the Qur'an; and (b) the precedence of Qur'anic instructions over those of the *ḥadīth*s in instances when the two are irreconcilable, are among the keys of Sharia hermeneutics of the existential framework.[15] This is because they are consistent with the notions of form and essence, given that the Qur'anic instructions are minimalistic and less contextual, and the instructions of *ḥadīth*s are maximalist and highly contextual.[16] In other words, the Qur'anic regulation is more 'essence-based', whereas the *ḥadīth*s formulate the same essence in and for differing existential contexts. Thus, the Qur'an is the first point of reference for the extrapolation of 'the essences' of the regulations contained within it, and a yardstick for understanding how the *ḥadīth*s have formulated these essences in differing contexts. For instance, consider the issue of the impurity of wine: there is no reference in the Qur'an of its impurity; the *ḥadīth*s, on the other hand, are at variance regarding its impurity.[17] In light of this, the *ḥadīth*s asserting the status of the purity of wine have precedence because they are congruent with the Qur'an, and those deeming wine to be an impure substance are taken as a means of deterring people from the consumption of wine – which is a prohibition of the Qur'an.[18]

---

13 Issues pertaining to the impurity of urine will be dealt with in due course.

14 See report no. 3 in al-Kulaynī, *Uṣūl al-Kāfī*, in *Mawsūʿat al-kutub al-arbaʿa fī aḥādīth al-nabī wa-l-ʿitra*, 1:350.

15 For the extrapolation of both rules, see Muḥammad Riḍā al-Muẓaffar, *Uṣūl al-fiqh* (Qum: Intishārāt Ismāʿīliyāt, 2004), 4:203–4.

16 This is alluded to in section 10 in al-Muẓaffar, *Uṣūl al-fiqh*, 1:142–3.

17 Issues pertaining to the impurity of wine will be dealt with in due course.

18 See Qur'an 5:90.

The traditional methods of: (a) *ḥadīth* reconciliation; (b) the preference of one *ḥadīth* over another; and (c) the nullification of both *ḥadīths* when conflict between them is irreconcilable, all of which render the majority of *ḥadīths* as ineffectual 'baggage', are not employed in the existential framework.[19] On the contrary, all *ḥadīths* are used as far as possible to determine how the essence of the regulation was formulated in differing contexts. This is in contrast to traditional scholarship which gives preference to some *ḥadīths* on the basis of their being 'the most authentic' when the *ḥadīth* texts conflict on the same subject, and hence only 'the most authentic' *ḥadīths* are employed in the derivation of regulations, after which they acquire the hallmark of 'generalisability'.[20] However, it is naïve to assume that the Prophet and Imāms did not instruct individuals on norms and issues in accordance with their respective capacities and contexts. The opposite is most certainly the case, and hence the existence of diverse instructions in *ḥadīth* literature vis-à-vis any given norm. All the diverse instructions pertaining to a particular issue share the same essence – they only differ in terms of their forms.

Aside from the general ethos of 'being clean', the stance of the Qur'an vis-à-vis the *fiqhī* (jurisprudentially) designated impure substances is silence. It does not even mention the prerequisite of 'ensuring the body and garments are cleansed of impurities' for devotional acts, nor the proscription of trading with impure substances. Accordingly, the Qur'anic position is deemed to be neutral with respect to impure substances. The implication of this 'neutrality' is that if the *ḥadīth* texts are inconclusive on: (a) the status of the impurity of, or (b) the prohibition of trading with, any of the Sharia-designated impure substances, then it will be concluded that they are pure (*ṭāhir*) in the Sharia sense. This is because the 'neutrality' or 'silence' of the Qur'an intervenes in such cases and adjudicates the state of ritual purity and/or permissibility of trade.[21]

19 For information on the traditional methods, see al-Muẓaffar, *Uṣūl al-fiqh*, 4:182–8, 197–204.

20 Ibid.

21 It should be noted that the precept of 'the neutrality of the Qur'an' in the existential framework is unrelated to 'the juristic maxim of the principality of purity' (*qaʿidat aṣālat al-ṭahāra* – everything is pure until you ascertain it is impure). This is because the latter bestows purity only to: (a) substances not listed in the category of 'impure substances' (*najāsāt*); and (b) objects speculated as having become contaminated (*mutanajjis*) due to potential contact with the listed impure substances. In other words, the status of purity conferred to a filthy substance unworthy of consumption by 'the principality of purity' merely signifies that its removal is not a prerequisite for devotional acts predicated upon a

6. Analysis of the Notions of *Najis* and *Najāsāt*

6.1 Etymology of the Word '*Najis*'

The word *najis* is an adjective of the root *na-ji-sa*, *na-ju-sa* and *na-ja-sa* whose literal significations include the meanings of the English words 'impure', 'unclean', 'dirty' and 'stained'.[22] Its antonym is *ṭāhir*, which is an adjective of the root *ṭa-hu-ra*, whose verbal noun, *ṭahāra*, literally signifies the English meanings of the words 'cleanliness', 'purity' and 'taintlessness'.[23] It is reported that when Imām 'Alī would cup water during the ritual ablutions he would say, 'Praise belongs to God who made water *ṭāhir* (clean) and not *najis* (dirty).'[24] The Qur'an frequently employs the word *ṭahūr* (excessively pure) as an adjective of rainwater to convey both its status as a 'clean' substance and its function as a purifier (*muṭahhir*).[25] The Qur'an also utilises the derivatives of the root *ṭa-hu-ra* in relation to ritual ablutions, and to depict the state of being free from character defects and the biological state of cleanliness post-menstruation.[26] In the Qur'an, the word *khabīth* and its derivatives are employed to signify the 'physical filth' of certain foodstuffs unworthy of consumption, and the word *rijs* is employed to signify the 'physical filth' of blood, dead animals and the flesh of swine.[27] However, it should be noted that the words *rijs* and *khabīth* and their derivatives are also employed by the Qur'an in other contexts to signify concepts not pertaining to physical filth.[28]

In today's Sharia convention, the word *najis* depicts a substance that is either impure in itself or becomes impure (*mutanajjis*) through contact with an impure substance via a medium whose property is wet.[29] It also denotes proscriptions

state of purity. For more information on *qa'idat aṣālat al-ṭahāra*, see al-Sayyid Muḥammad Kāẓim al-Muṣṭafawī, *al-Qawā'id* (Qum: Mu'assasat Nashr al-Islāmī, 2008), 156–8.

22 Hans Wehr, *Arabic-English Dictionary* (United States: Spoken Languages Services, 1994), 1109.

23 For the English meanings, see Wehr, *Arabic-English Dictionary*, 667. For the fact that it is the antonym of *najis*/*najāsa*, see E. W. Lane, *Arabic-English Lexicon* (Cambridge: The Islamic Texts Society, 2003), 2:2770.

24 See report no. 1. in Ibn Bābawayh al-Qummī, *Man lā yaḥḍaruhu al-faqīh*, in *Mawsū'at al-kutub al-arba'a fī aḥādīth al-nabī wa-l-'itra*, 1:97.

25 See Qur'an 25:48.

26 See Qur'an 5:6, 3:42 and 2:222.

27 See Qur'an 7:157 and 6:145.

28 For instance, see Qur'an 8:38 and 9:125.

29 See Mirzā 'Alī al-Mishkīnī, *Muṣṭalaḥāt al-fiqh* (Beirut: Manshūrāt al-Riḍā, 2010), 529–32.

with respect to that substance in the domains of obligatory devotional acts and trade.[30] This means that, in addition to the requirement of keeping the body, garments and places of worship free from impure substances, the state of 'being cleansed' of such substances is also a pre-requisite condition of all obligatory devotional acts, such as *ṣalāt* and circumambulation around the Ka'ba (*ṭawāf*). Among the proscriptions associated with impure substances designated as *najis* is the prohibition of their consumption, which classifies as a 'normative regulation' (*ḥukm taklīfī*). The prohibition of a *najis* substance in relation to the performance of devotional acts classifies as a 'status-based regulation' (*ḥukm waḍ'ī*); and the prohibition of trading with it classifies as both a 'normative' and a 'status-based' regulation. This means that: (a) the consumption of *najis* substances results in sin; (b) the performance of obligatory devotional acts with either *najis* clothes or the presence of *najis* substances on the body are rendered invalid; and (c) trading with such substances is both invalid and results in sin.

It should be noted that the extensions of the category of impure substances (*najāsāt*), necessitating such connotations of 'invalidity' and 'sin' in the domains of obligatory devotional acts and trade, are limited to those defined by the Sharia. The category does not include all substances generally considered 'dirty'. Hence, only urine, stool, semen, blood, sweat of an excrement-eating animal, pigs, dogs, wine, dead bodies and non-Muslims qualify as extensions of the category of impure substances.[31] All other 'dirty' substances, such as pus and mud, do not.[32]

6.2 The Notions of *Najis* and *Najāsāt* in the Qur'an and *Hādīths*

As mentioned above, the Qur'an does not explicitly reference the items considered impure (*najis*) by today's Sharia convention as 'impure substances' (*najāsāt*). Similarly, it does not state that trading with them is prohibited, or

30 Ibid.

31 Ibid, 531–32.

32 According to Sunnī scholars, most types of pus and vomit are impure substances defiling objects that come into contact with them. See Ze'ev Maghen, 'Close Encounters: Some Preliminary Observations on the Transmission of Impurity in Early Sunnī Jurisprudence', *Islamic Law and Society* 6, no. 3 (1999): 361–2; and Richard Gauvain, 'Ritual Rewards: A Consideration of Three Recent Approaches to Sunni Purity Law', *Islamic Law and Society* 12, no. 3 (2005): 359–60.

that obligatory devotional acts are contingent upon the prerequisite condition of 'the body and garments being pure or cleansed of the Sharia-designated impure substances'. The statements pertaining to physical purity in the Qur'an are general, such as: 'Cleanse your garments!' and: 'Allah loves those who cleanse themselves!'[33] As regards the prerequisites of devotional acts, the Qur'an only mentions the necessity of ceremonial purity (*ṭahāra*) prior to performing the daily obligatory prayers (*ṣalawāt*) after waking from sleep, visiting the lavatory and sexual intercourse. It stipulates the minor ablution (*wuḍū'*), lustration (*ghusl*), or their dry substitute (*tayyamum*) as means of acquiring this ceremonial purity.[34]

The reports of the Prophet include questions posed to him regarding the method of purifying garments and the body of unclean substances, such as blood and urine, in the general context of everydayness, and not merely in light of the daily obligatory prayers.[35] They also include instructions to women on how to cleanse garments sullied by menstrual blood prior to resuming the daily obligatory prayers.[36] Clearly, the primary function of the reports of this genre, when viewed collectively, is to affirm and emphasise the aforementioned Qur'anic dictum of the necessity of being clean and free of the impure substances in the context of everydayness. Additionally, the questions posed to the Prophet reveal that the people already knew or had an idea about which substances classified as impure substances.[37] In fact, the usages of the word *najis* and other derivatives of the root *na-ja-sa* in these early texts do not have the implicative sense they carry today of the necessity of ensuring a state of being cleansed from certain substances as a prerequisite to certain acts of devotions or entering a mosque.[38] Thus, the most that can be derived from the Qur'an and Prophetic *ḥadīth*s is the necessity to be clean of things considered filthy and unclean in the context of everydayness with particular emphasis on certain substances, such as blood and urine. Regarding the prohibition of trading

33 See Qur'an 74:4, 9:108 and 2:222.

34 See Qur'an 5:6.

35 See al-'Āmilī, *Tafṣīl wasā'il al-shī'a*, 3:395–429.

36 See al-'Āmilī, *Tafṣīl wasā'il al-shī'a*, 2:271–369.

37 For instance, see reports regarding urine in *Kitāb al-wuḍū'*, and reports in *Kitāb al-ghusl* and *Kitāb al-ḥayḍ* in al-Bukhārī, *Ṣaḥīḥ al-Bukhārī* (Beirut: Dār al-Fikr, 1994), 1:68–72 and 76–97.

38 See sections of *ṭahāra* in *Mawsū'at al-kutub al-arba'a fī aḥādīth al-nabī wa-l-'itra*. In fact, very few derivatives of the root *na-ja-sa* are employed in the corpus of these canonical works.

with impure substances, there is a report of the Prophet stating that when God prohibits a thing, He similarly prohibits its price.[39] The implication here is that in addition to the prohibition of consuming such 'prohibited' substances, such as swine and wine, their sale is similarly prohibited.[40]

The reports of the fifth and sixth Imāms offer a fuller elaboration of the substances and entities classifying as impure substances (*najāsāt*) with explicit reference to the contexts of devotions and trade.[41] The word *najis* is employed in a few reports referring to dogs and 'an enemy of the Prophet's family' (*nāṣibī*), whereas the majority of reports utilise other words connoting 'dirtiness', 'filthiness', 'unworthiness' and 'unwholesomeness', such as *qadhir* and *khabatha*.[42]

It is important to note that the source of the designation of certain substances as 'impure' is the *ḥadīth* literature. However, the connotation carried by the terms *najis* and *najāsāt* as 'things that must be cleansed as per the Sharia, as opposed to 'things that are merely dirty', is the outcome of later jurisprudential deliberations.[43] With the passage of time the words *najis* and *ṭāhir* became associated with each other as antonyms in the *fiqhī* discourse. The effect of this was the transfer of meaning of the word *najis* from an adjective merely describing things as dirty (as opposed to clean) to an adjective signifying that substances must be cleansed for the accurate and valid execution of certain devotions, such as the daily obligatory prayers.[44] Thus, there is no doubt that the Sharia meaning of the word *najis* (and hence its derivatives) was not its 'associated meaning' (*ma'nā bi-l-tabādur*) during the revelatory era (*al-haqīqa al-shar'iyya*).[45] In fact, it is impossible to glean the Sharia meaning from the early Shī'ī *ḥadīth* literature.[46] In any case, it is certain that the change of meaning

39 See report no. 301 in al-Aḥsā'ī, *'Awālī al-li'ālī* (Qum: Maṭba'a Sayyid al-Shuhadā' 'Alayhi al-Salām, 1983), 2:110.

40 It should be noted that such 'prohibited' substances are only prohibited on the basis of their relations to human beings. In and of themselves, and in relation to other than humans, they are pure and have existential significance and purpose.

41 See for instance chapters on the prohibition of sale of the various *najāsāt*, such as pig, dog and wine in al-'Āmilī, *Tafṣīl wasā'il al-shī'a*, 17:118–120 and 223–7.

42 For the utility of the word *najis* with regards to the *nāṣibī*, see report no. 5 in al-'Āmilī, *Tafṣīl wasā'il al-shī'a*, 1:220. For the utility of words other than *najis* to signify filth, see sections of *ṭahāra* in *Mawsū'a al-kutub al-arba'a fī aḥādīth al-nabī wa-l-'itra*.

43 See footnote 39.

44 See al-Mishkīnī, *Muṣṭalaḥāt al-fiqh*, 531–32.

45 *Al-haqīqa al-shar'iyya* refers to the fact that the transfer of the meaning of a word occurred during the revelatory era. See Muẓaffar, *Uṣūl al-fiqh*, 1:37–39.

46 See footnote 39. Moreover, none of the canonical works of *ḥadīth* have sections on

occurred outside of the revelatory era (*al-haqīqa al-mutasharri'iyya*).[47] This transference of meaning of the terms *najis* and *najāsāt*, and their subsequent application to certain substances in jurisprudence, has resulted in a number of absurd supplementary beliefs that will of necessity – if not readily – be assented to by the majority of Shī'ī Muslims, such as the following example: a hand covered with mud and pus is pure (*ṭāhir*) in itself, whereas a hand that has come in contact with a wet dog or the tears of an infidel is absolutely impure.[48]

6.3 Cleanliness and Hygiene in the Context of Pre-Islamic Arabia

Qur'anic verses and Prophetic reports exhorting the necessity of purity, purification, and cleanliness – such as, 'God loves those who cleanse themselves!', 'Cleanse your garments!', and, 'Cleanliness is half of faith!' –[49] must be analysed in the context of the lifestyle and hostile desert environment of the Arabs of the revelatory contexts. The Qur'an and *ḥadīth* literature portrays the context as one in which animal sacrifices and the veneration of blood were ingrained norms inherited from pre-Islamic cultures.[50] Additionally, there was a total lack of attention and awareness vis-à-vis sanitation, washing, changing dirty garments, and consuming dead animals, or food contaminated by dead rats.[51] Such norms are detrimental to the physical aspect of the human being, and inconducive to the actualisation of the moral and spiritual facets of the soul. Thus, it was necessary to introduce strict protocols on cleanliness to shift the mindset of the people, instituting a novel and contextually appropriate paradigm conducive to the growth of the individual and community.

---

najāsa found in the later *ḥadīth* compilations.

47 *Al-haqīqa al-mutasharri'iyya* refers to the fact that the transfer of the meaning of a word occurred outside of the revelatory era, that is, a word's 'new' meaning became its associated meaning for the adherents of the Sharia at some point after the revelatory era. See al-Muẓaffar, *Uṣūl al-fiqh*, 1:37–39.

48 See footnote 32 for the Sunnī take on the purity status of pus and vomit.

49 See Qur'an 74:4 and 9:108 for the first two quotes. The last quote is a portion of a famous report of the Prophet, see report 223 in *Kitāb al-ṭahāra* in Ibn Muslim al-Nīsābūrī, *Ṣaḥīḥ Muslim* (Cairo: Dār al-Āfāk al-'Arabiyya, 2005), 111.

50 See Qur'an 16:115 and 5:2–3, and sections of *ṭahāra* and *aṭ'ima* in *Mawsū'a al-kutub al-arba'a fī aḥādīth al-nabī wa-l-'itra*. For instance, there are many reports dealing with the issue of the consumption of mud in al-Kulaynī, *Furū' al-Kāfī*, 6:280–1.

51 Again, this can be surmised from sections of *ṭahāra* and *aṭ'ima* in *Mawsū'a al-kutub al-arba'a fī aḥādīth al-nabī wa-l-'itra*.

The introduction of lustration (*ghusl*) on Fridays and other occasions, the instructions to wear fresh garments for prayers preferably with perfume, and the constant encouragement of brushing one's teeth to the extent that the Prophet refrained from consuming foods causing bad breath, are a few examples of the innovative norms indicative of this endeavour to change the pagan Arab mindset.[52] However, this did not mean that the presence of impure substances on the body or garments was absolutely intolerable in the general context of everydayness or even during the daily prayers, as will be discussed in the next sections; rather, the prophetic approach was measured and within reason.

7. The Regulation of the Impurity of Non-Muslims

Despite the numerous derivatives of the root of the word *najis* in the Arabic language, the Qur'an mentions only one, which is employed just once. The word *najas* (filthy) is used to describe the polytheists of Mecca in the penultimate chapter revealed chronologically, that is, towards the end of the revelatory era: 'Indeed the polytheists are impure (*najas*). Thus, let them not come near the Sacred Mosque (*masjid al- ḥarām*) after this year' (Q9:28). To reiterate, this is the only utility of any of the derivatives of the root of the word *najis* in the Qur'an. It should be noted that this verse is not the point of origin of the Shīʿī Imāmī notion of the communicability of the impurity of the non-Muslim to other objects or people, rather it is a 'retroactive justification', as David Freidenreich aptly puts it.[53] He states that, unlike the Torah, the Qur'an is spiritually 'egalitarian' in that each human 'has equal access to the holiness that comes from being in relationship with God'.[54] It does not discriminate on the basis of religious or sectarian identity, for it postulates that salvation is available to every member of every community.[55] Thus, he asserts that it is: 'the interpretation of Qur'an exclusively in light of... post-Qur'anic works that yields a strained understanding of the Qur'an's own discourse on impurity.'[56]

52 For instance, see al-Ṭūsī, *al-Istibṣār*, in *Mawsūʿat al-kutub al-arbaʿa fī aḥādīth al-nabī wa-l-ʿitra* (Beirut: Dār al-Taʿāruf li-l-Maṭbūʿāt, 1998), 1:97–104, 174–194.

53 D. Freidenreich, 'The Implications of Unbelief: Tracing the Emergence of Distinctively Shiʿi Notions Regarding the Food and Impurity of Non-Muslims', *Islamic Law and Society* 18, no. 1 (2011): 53–6.

54 David Freidenreich, 'Holiness and Impurity in the Torah and the Quran: Differences within a Common Typology', *Comparative Islamic Studies* 6, no. 6.1–6.2 (2011): 5.

55 See Qur'an 2:62 and 5:69.

56 Freidenreich, 'Holiness and Impurity in the Torah and the Quran', 11–13.

This section of the paper presents the Shīʿī and Sunnī perspectives on the purity status of the non-Muslim including a brief overview of the evolution of the Shīʿī position. It then provides the reason for the difference between the Shīʿī and Sunnī views. The section concludes with an existential critique of the Shīʿī juristic reasoning behind the derivation of the regulation of the impurity of the non-Muslim.

7.1 Shīʿī Imāmī and Sunnī Positions on the Purity Status of the Non-Muslim

Both Shīʿī and Sunnī *fiqhī* discourses discuss the purity status of the clean bodies of non-Muslims extensively; however, there is no consensus between them regarding the impurity of non-Muslims.[57] The terminology employed in their respective *fiqhī* literatures pertaining to the discourse of impure substances is generally the same: *najāsa ḥaqīqiyya/ḥissiyya* refers to real or sensorial impurity and *najāsa maʿnawiyya/ḥukmiyya* to spiritual or legal impurity.[58]

7.2 The Sunnī Position

Sunnī Islam is perhaps the 'only religious purity code' which asserts that humans are not essentially impure, and that their physical bodies are not able to transfer impurity to other people or objects.[59] Humans are intrinsically pure organisms, hence the polytheist (*mushrik*) and unbeliever (*kāfir*) are not intrinsically impure (*najis al-dhāt*) like pigs, blood or urine, rather they are intrinsically pure (*ṭāhir al-dhāt*).[60] This means they can never be contagiously impure.[61] Thus, regardless whether the contaminating form of impurity (*najāsa*) is physical or spiritual, it cannot render the essence of the human impure.[62] Sunnī scholars only regard those objects that communicate impurity to other

57 Ze'ev Maghen, 'Strangers and Brothers: The Ritual Status of Unbelievers in Islamic Jurisprudence', *Medieval encounters* 12, no. 2 (2006): 176–9.

58 Ze'ev Maghen, 'First Blood: Purity, Edibility, and the Independence of Islamic Jurisprudence', *Der Islam* 81, no. 1 (2004): 51. See also Mishkīnī, *Muṣṭalaḥāt al-fiqh*, 529–32.

59 Maghen, 'Close Encounters', 350.

60 Ibid., 364.

61 Gauvain, 'Ritual Rewards', 359.

62 Maghen, 'Close Encounters', 364.

objects as intrinsically impure (*najis al-dhāt*).[63] Hence, since saliva issues from the essence of the creature, the saliva of dogs is impure because dogs are essentially impure, whereas the saliva of humans is pure because humans are essentially pure.[64] This position – that all human beings, including women and non-Muslims, are essentially pure – stems from the creation narratives in which all humans are subject to the Fall, and so all of them are equally pure and equally lacking.[65]

Sunnī scholars do not regard the word *najas* in Q9:28 as denoting physical bodily impurity (*najāsa*), rather it signifies internal impurity due to erroneous beliefs. They maintain that if it did denote bodily impurity, then the Qur'an would not have permitted marriage with *ahl al-kitāb*, and the Prophet would not have had such free and convivial relations with them.[66]

7.3 The Shīʿī Imāmī Position

The physical impurity of polytheists (*mushrikūn*), by which is meant all non-Muslims, is unique to Shīʿī *fiqhī* discourse.[67] The majority of scholars consider all non-Muslims, which includes the *ahl al-kitāb*, as both 'impure' and 'polluting'.[68] Interestingly, out of all the schools of *fiqh*, it is the Shīʿī Imāmī school that has devised the most elaborate taxonomy for the unbeliever (*kāfir*).[69] People who classify as 'ritually

63 Ibid., 368.

64 Ibid., 363.

65 Gauvain, 'Ritual Rewards', 383.

66 Ibid., 379, footnote 141.

67 Maghen, 'Much Ado about *Wuḍū*'', 226. For instance, in al-Ṭūsī, *al-Istibṣār* 4:87–93 and 3:184–187, all reports pertaining to: (a) the slaughter of meat of the Majūs, Christians, and Jews are subsumed under the title of *Bāb dhabā'iḥ al-kuffār*; and (b) marriage to the Majūs, Christians, and Jews are subsumed under the title of *Bāb taḥrīm nikāḥ al-kawāfir min sā'ir aṣnāf al-kuffār*.

68 Safran, 'Rules of Purity and Confessional Boundaries', 201.

69 Maghen, 'Strangers and Brothers', 180. For instance, the Shīʿī taxonomy for the unbeliever includes: (a) *kāfir dhimmī*, an unbeliever living in the Abode of Islam; (b) *kāfir ḥarbī*, an unbeliever living in the Abode of War; (c) *kāfir murtadd*, an apostate which is of two types – (c-i) *murtadd fiṭrī*, an apostate whose parents were Muslim, and (c-ii) *murtadd millī*, an apostate who was a Muslim convert; (d) *ghulāt*, a theological exaggerator; (e) Khawārij, seceders; and (f) *nawāṣib*, those who hate the *ahl al-bayt*. This list is not exhaustive. See ibid.

impure', such as Buddhists, are contagious vis- à -vis their impurity.[70] In other words, the unbeliever (*kāfir*) is listed among those Sharia-designated impure substances that can transfer impurity to a Shīʿī Imāmī via contact.[71]

There is no dispute among the Shīʿī scholars with respect to all non-Muslims (*mushrikīn*) being spiritually impure (*najis maʿnawī*). However, the notion of their physical bodies being impure (*ʿayn al-najāsa*) has gradually evolved from uncertainty and debate, to unanimity amongst the scholars.[72] From the fifth century onwards, the people of the Book were designated as *kāfir* in Shīʿī *fiqhī* literature and hence impure. It is at this point that Qur'an 9:28 is employed as the basis and justification for this designation, and the notion of non-Muslim impurity shifts from being a negative state of mind to actual physical impurity that is tangible and communicable via physical contact. Thus, the Shīʿī *fiqhī* literature mentions all types of additional restrictions previously never instated.[73] These include the prohibitions of marrying them and consuming their food, contradicting the permissibility of both expressed in Qur'an 5:5.[74] Due to the fact that such Qur'anic verses presuppose the purity of the people of the Book, scholars dedicated an inordinate number of pages to 'eisegetical' interpretations of such verses in order to nullify the explicit permissibility of marrying them and partaking of their food.[75] Historically, this classification of *ahl al-kitāb* as 'unbelievers' (and hence impure) led to a host of prejudicial regulations in other domains of governance, such as inheritance, in Shīʿī Imāmī polities post fifth century.[76]

70 T. G. Tabrizi, 'Ritual Purity and Buddhists in Modern Twelver Shi'a Exegesis and Law', *Journal of Shi'a Islamic Studies* 5, no. 4 (2012): 456.

71 Tsadik, 'The Legal Status of Religious Minorities', 382. For the complete listing of the impure substances, see al-Mishkīnī, *Muṣṭalaḥāt al-fiqh*, 531–32.

72 Maghen, 'Strangers and Brothers', 181–2.

73 David M. Freidenreich, 'Christians in Early and Classical Shīʿī Law', in *Christian-Muslim Relations. A Bibliographical History. Volume 3 (1050-1200)*, 33–35. Brill, 2011.

74 Tsadik, 'The Legal Status of Religious Minorities', 386.

75 Ibid. 387–8. Since the majority of Shīʿī scholars classified *ahl al-kitāb* as 'unbelievers', they considered only 'temporary' marriage to them as legitimate. Very few Shīʿī scholars regarded 'permanent' marriage to *ahl al-kitāb* as valid. Others asserted that both 'permanent' and 'temporary' marriages to them were invalid.

76 Ibid. 389.

Among the conclusions of the Shīʿī position of the impurity of non-Muslims are: 1) non-Muslims are contagious and can transmit impurity by physical contact especially via a wet medium; 2) the clothing of non-Muslims is impure; 3) the utensils and food of non-Muslims is prohibited; and 4) marriage to non-Muslim women is forbidden.[77]

It should be noted that there are numerous reports of the Imāms purporting the contrary view, that is, the physical purity of the non-Muslim.[78] As will be discussed, often the hesitation expressed on the part of the Imāms regarding the consumption of the food of the 'other' was in light of certain culinary conventions of non-Muslims, such as the consumption of wine and pork, and the possibility of their food being contaminated by them.[79] Hence, there have always been a minority of scholars (in every generation) who argued for the purity of non-Muslims, that is, unbelievers, polytheists and *ahl al-kitāb*.[80]

7.4 Evolution of the Shīʿī Imāmī Position on the Purity Status of the Non-Muslim

The *ḥadīth* literature pertaining to this issue is ambiguous when taken as a whole because it purports both the purity and impurity of non-Muslims. It neither unanimously regards all non-Muslims to have the same purity status, nor does it consistently accord them the capacity to communicate their impurity.[81] The notion of 'the impurity of the non-Muslim' and its communicability emerges over time. It becomes established as the de facto position of the Shīʿī Imāmī community in the fifth century.[82] It is at this point that Qur'an 9:28

77 Maghen, 'Strangers and Brothers', 187.

78 In all four canonical works of ḥadith, there are numerous reports in all sections pertaining to non-Muslims presupposing the physical purity of non-Muslims. See, for instance, reports in: (a) al-Ṭūsī, *al-Istibṣār*, 4:90–92; and (b) al-Ṭūsī, *Tahdhīb al-aḥkām*, 9:64–65.

79 Maghen, 'Strangers and Brothers', 192.

80 For instance, see Tsadik, 'The Legal Status of Religious Minorities', 382. Here, Tsadik cites a few scholars of the thirteenth/nineteenth and fourteenth/twentieth centuries who asserted the purity of non-Muslims.

81 Freidenreich, 'The Implications of Unbelief', 55.

82 Freidenreich, 'Christians in Early and Classical Shīʿī Law', 34. Here, Freidenreich states that no consensus existed among Shīʿī scholars prior to the fifth century on the three essential characteristics of the post-fifth century notion of non-Muslim impurity: 'its universality, communicability and relationship to unbelief'.

is utilised as an evidence for 'the impurity of the non-Muslim'.[83] Hence, the examination of *ḥadīth* literature and works of scholars of the third, fourth and fifth centuries reveal a gradual shift in Shīʿī Imāmī thought regarding the purity of the non-Muslims.[84]

Shīʿī *fiqhī* literature of the third century is indicative of the existence of a phase in which scholars distinguished between the purity status of *ahl al-kitāb* and other non-Muslims; that is, they did not view Christians and Jews as impure.[85] Their position would have been informed by reports of the Imāms presupposing the non-communicability of all non-Muslims.[86] It seems that prior to the fifth century, the majority of Shīʿī scholars did not consider non-Muslims to be inherently impure, rather the cause for the prohibition of consuming the food of non-Muslims was understood to be the possibility of their food being contaminated by wine and pork, as per numerous reports of the Imāms.[87]

The gradual evolution of the Shīʿī notion of non-Muslim impurity – from being a non-communicable inner state to a communicable and intrinsic property of the body – is discernible in the changing Shīʿī attitudes towards the consumption of meat slaughtered by non-Muslims. Shīʿī scholars of the second and third centuries mirror their Sunnī contemporaries by distinguishing between meat slaughtered by *ahl al-kitāb* and meat slaughtered by other non-Muslims, the former being permissible. Some Shīʿī Imāmī scholars of the third and fourth centuries stated there was no difference between meat slaughtered

83 Freidenreich, 'The Implications of Unbelief', 55 and 79.

84 Freidenreich, 'Christians in Early and Classical Shīʿī Law', 36.

85 Freidenreich, 'The Implications of Unbelief', 71. These early scholars distinguished between the people of the Book and Zoroastrians, where only the latter were considered a source of impurity. Other early scholars did not consider the impurity of non-Muslims as communicable at all. Yet others stated that the communicability of impurity was not caused by improper beliefs but the improper behaviours of non-Muslims, such as wine and pork consumption, whereby there was a possibility of contamination of food and clothing with the impure substances. These scholars maintained that it was possible to consume the food of Christians, Jews and Zoroastrians so long as they purified themselves by performing the ritual ablutions prior to the preparation of food. Thus, early Shīʿī scholars had a diverse spectrum of opinions just like those of their Sunnī contemporaries. See Freidenreich, 'Christians in Early and Classical Shīʿī Law', 33–35.

86 Freidenreich, 'The Implications of Unbelief', 72. Also, see reports in al-ʿĀmilī, *Tafṣīl wasāʾil al-shīʿa*, 3:518–20.

87 Freidenreich, 'The Implications of Unbelief', 74. Also, see: (a) report no. 107 in Ibn Bābawayh al-Qummī, *Man lā yaḥḍaruhu al-faqīh*, 3:214. (b) reports in al-Ṭūsī, *Tahdhīb al-aḥkām*, 9:81.

by *ahl al-kitāb* and other non-Muslims. Hence, some scholars permitted the consumption of meat slaughtered by all non-Muslims so long as the butchers invoked the name of God prior to the slaughtering; others prohibited it because all non-Muslim butchers were incapable of reciting the name of God properly by virtue of their 'non-Muslimness'. At the turn of the fifth century, Shīʿī Imāmī scholars from Shaykh al-Mufīd onwards chose to adopt the more restrictive of these verdicts. Additionally, there was a shift in understanding regarding the cause of the prohibition: scholars of the previous centuries asserted the cause as being the inability of non-Muslim butchers to ritually slaughter animals correctly, whereas Mufīd, his students and subsequent scholars emphasised the cause as being solely erroneous belief.[88]

The same evolutionary trend is discernible regarding Shīʿī Imāmī attitudes towards marrying non-Muslims. In the second century, marriage to *ahl al-kitāb* was permitted. By the fourth century, the prevalent attitude had changed: Ibn Bābawayh states that all such marriages were disgraceful but permissible. In the fifth century, Mufīd, his students and subsequent Shīʿī scholars declare all marriages with non-Muslims as prohibited because of their false beliefs, and hence their impurity.[89] However, they did not entirely reject the distinction between *ahl al-kitāb* and other non-Muslims. Mufīd permitted taking Jewish and Christian concubines but prohibited taking all other non-Muslim concubines. His student, Shaykh Ṭūsī, consolidated and clarified the issue for the Shīʿī community by declaring: (a) the prohibition of 'permanent' marriage to *ahl al-kitāb*; (b) the permissibility of 'temporary' marriage to them; (c) the disapproval (*karāha*) of temporary marriage to Zoroastrians (*majūs*); and (d) the prohibition of 'temporary' marriage to the *nāṣibī* (the hater of the family of the Prophet).[90] Another of Mufīd's student, the renowned al-Sharif al-Murtaḍā, was the first Shīʿī authority to use Qur'an 9:28 as the basis and justification for the essential impurity of non-Muslims.[91]

88 Freidenreich, 'Christians in Early and Classical Shīʿī Law', 36. For the diversity of reports on the issue of the slaughter of meat by non-Muslims, see: (a) al-Ṭūsī, *Tahdhīb al-aḥkām*, 9:59–65. (b) al-Kulaynī, *Furūʿ al-Kāfī*, 6:251–5. (c) al-Ṭūsī, *al-Istibṣār*, 4:87–93. (d) Ibn Bābawayh al-Qummī, *Man lā yaḥḍaruhu al-faqīh*, 3:205.

89 For a sample of the diversity of reports pertaining to the issue of marriage to non-Muslims, see reports in: (a) al-Ṭūsī, *Tahdhīb al-aḥkām*, 7:266–7. (b) al-Kulaynī, *Furūʿ al-Kāfī*, 5:361–3. (c) al-Ṭūsī, *al-Istibṣār*, 3:184–7. (d) Ibn Bābawayh al-Qummī, *Man lā yaḥḍaruhu al-faqīh*, 3:252–3.

90 Freidenreich, 'Christians in Early and Classical Shīʿī Law', 39.

91 Freidenreich, 'The Implications of Unbelief', 76–8.

The Safavid period marks the point of total consolidation of the view of the physical impurity of the non-Muslim in Imāmī Shīʿism. The venerated Safavid scholar, Muḥammad Bāqir al-Majlisī, was a key contributor to the eventual domination of this view, and his works serve as an important record of the attitudes towards the 'other' amongst the Shīʿī scholars since the fifth century.[92] He cites the arguments of formative scholars, such as Ṭūsī, who spent considerable effort trying to discount all authentic reports of the Imāms signifying the cause of the prohibition of consuming the food of *ahl al-kitāb* as being the possibility of its contamination with pork or wine. Such reports, which are significant in number, were problematic for these scholars as they did not support their thesis of the cause being the communicability of impurity of the bodies of *ahl al-kitāb*. Hence, they offered a host of possible meanings to the Imāms' words with a view to discounting them on the basis that the Imāms must have been in the state of 'dissimulation' (*taqiyya*);[93] even though there was no precedence for such a conclusion amongst the scholars of the second, third and fourth centuries who examined these very same reports and asserted contrary conclusions or justifications.[94] Majlisī took it upon himself to explain away Qur'anic verses permitting full social interaction with *ahl al-kitāb*, such as Qur'an 5:5.[95] By the end of the Safavid period, the overwhelming majority of scholars were of the opinion that non-Muslims were impure both spiritually and physically, and that: 'Their essences/persons are ritually unclean like those of dogs and hogs.'[96]

The position of the physical impurity of all non-Muslims was the dominant and prevalent view amongst scholars until the twentieth century. Despite some very notable scholars of the twentieth century asserting the physical purity of non-Muslims, they were overshadowed by the two foremost Shīʿī jurists of the contemporary era, Ayatollahs Khūʾī and Khumaynī, who maintained the impurity status of all non-Muslims. Hence, it continued to be the part of the worldview of the majority Shīʿī Imāmī Muslims throughout the twentieth century and is not uncommon today.[97]

92 Maghen, 'Strangers and Brothers', 181–2.

93 Ibid., 183.

94 Freidenreich, 'Christians in Early and Classical Shīʿī Law', 33–37.

95 Maghen, 'Strangers and Brothers', 184.

96 Ibid., 187.

97 Ibid., 190. As mentioned in footnote 12, the impurity of non-Muslims was the official verdict of both Ayatollahs Khūʾī and Khumaynī; however their advanced classes in *fiqh* and their elaborated *fiqhī* works (*al-fiqh al-istidlālī*) present arguments and justifications

7.5 Reason for the Difference Between the Shīʿī Imāmī and Sunnī Position

The Sunnī purity code is extremely lenient in comparison to the Shīʿī.[98] A pertinent question asked by academics studying the issue of the purity status of non-Muslims in both Shīʿī and Sunnī *fiqhī* literatures is: why have the Shīʿī authorities adopted such a draconian stance? Goldziher contends it may have been due to Zoroastrian influence; however, such a claim is unjustified due to lack of evidence. Freidenreich offers the most likely answer: Shīʿī authorities from the fifth century onwards wished to distinguish themselves from Sunnīs, and hence adopted the contrary position to them, as they did on many other regulative issues.[99]

Both Shīʿī and Sunnī regulative systems view Christians and Jews as *dhimmīs*, a term signifying second-class citizenship under Muslim rule; however. in terms of their beliefs, the Shīʿī classify them as '*kāfir*' (unbelievers whose religion is unacceptable to God), whereas the Sunnī classify them as '*kitābī*' (adherents of a religion based on divinely revealed scripture).[100] The function of designating *ahl al-kitāb* as *kāfir*, according to Freidenreich, is not to assert or emphasise the difference between Muslims and non-Muslims because this was achieved by the term *dhimmī*; rather, its function was to stress differences between the beliefs and practices of the Shīʿī and Sunnī.[101] By applying the designation of *kāfir* to *ahl al-kitāb*, Shīʿī scholars intended to proclaim the

---

to the contrary, the essence of which are utilised in this paper.

98 Gauvain, 'Ritual Rewards', 390. In fact, Gauvain asserts that the Sunnī purity code is more lenient and prayer focussed than the purity codes of other religions too.

99 Freidenreich, 'The Implications of Unbelief', 80–2. For instance, see al-Sharīf al-Murtaḍā's *al-Intiṣār*, a polemical work arguing for the superiority of Shīʿī legal norms over Sunnī ones. (Freidenreich, 'Christians in Early and Classical Shīʿī Law', 35).

100 Ibid., 28.

101 Ibid., 30–35. Here, Freidenreich states that the regulations pertaining to *dhimmīs* within the Shīʿī regulative system, such as in the domains of property, finances, inheritance and criminality, are very similar to the regulations pertaining to *dhimmīs* within the Sunnī regulative systems. There are no significant differences between them – both are equally unfair and restrictive of *dhimmīs* in their respective legislations. The function of the *dhimmī* regulations is merely to delineate the non-Muslim as socially and legally inferior to the Muslim. It should be noted that there is a difference between Shīʿī and Sunnī regulations pertaining to monetary restitution, such as 'the blood money', due to the distinctions Sunnī scholars make within the non-Muslim category, such as between the people of the Book and the Zoroastrians.

superiority of their beliefs and practices over those of the Sunnī, thus rendering the latter's as being defective and corrupted.[102] They maintained that the failure of Sunnī scholars to acknowledge the full implications of the unbelief of *ahl al-kitāb* had inevitable consequences on the purity status of Sunnīs and the efficacy of their worship.[103] In light of this, Freidenreich (and other western academics) conclude that the Shīʿī discourse on the impurity of all non-Muslims is not actually about non-Muslims; rather, it is an opportunity to stress which Muslims are truly following the will of God.[104]

7.6 Existential Critique of the Shīʿī Imāmī Juristic Reasoning

Traditional Shīʿī jurisprudential (*fiqhī*) discourse regards the predicative adjective *najas* in Qur'an 9:28 as the cause of the banishment of the polytheists from Mecca and/or the vicinity of the Sacred Mosque.[105] On the whole, legists

102 Ibid., 29. To illustrate that scholars classified the people of the book as *kāfir*, Freidenreich refers to Mufīd's verdict that the *jizya* (a special tax for *dhimmī*s) is incumbent upon all *kuffār ahl al-kitāb* (the scripturist unbelievers) which includes Zoroastrians. Later, al-Ṭūsī clarified that Zoroastrians are not scripturist but have the same *kāfir* status. (Ibid.) The approach of Sunnī scholars was to downplay the practical ramifications of the impurity of the non-Muslim, whereas from the fifth century onwards the Shīʿī scholars have done the opposite. See ibid., 30–35.

103 Ibid., 35. Freidenreich continues that the thesis that Shīʿī scholars from the fifth century onwards devised the notion of non-Muslim impurity to distinguish themselves from the Sunnī community, may be evinced from the discourse pertaining to the impurity of the foods of the non-Muslims. This is because it is frequently accompanied by anti-Sunnī polemic. (Ibid., 36.) Consider the following example: Sunnī scholars distinguished the food of *ahl al-kitāb* from the food of other non-Muslims with respect to animal slaughter. (D. M. Freidenreich, 'The Food of the Damned', in *Between Heaven and Hell: Islam, Salvation, and the Fate of Others*, ed. M. H. Khalil [New York: Oxford University Press, 2013], 257.). According to them, the former is permissible to consume as per Qur'an 5:5. They viewed the Qur'anic permission as an expression of the affinity between Muslims and the people of the book. In contrast to this, Shīʿī scholars from the fifth century onwards saw no such affinity. (Freidenreich, 'Christians in Early and Classical Shīʿī Law', 36.). They asserted that Sunnī scholars permitting the consumption of meat slaughtered and prepared by *ahl al-kitāb*, was evidence of their non-faithfulness to the proper teachings of Islam. In this regard, al-Mufīd was very hostile towards Sunnīs stating that they were evil and tyrannical, and desirous of the persecution of pious Shīʿīs. (Ibid. 37.)

104 Freidenreich, 'The Food of the Damned', 261.

105 See al-Ṭabāṭabāʾī, *Mabānī minhāj al-ṣāliḥīn*, 3:244–8.

endeavour to justify the assumption that polytheism causes the body of the polytheist and its fluids to become impure.[106] Hence polytheists are prohibited from entering Mecca and/or the sacred mosque because impure objects cannot be permitted into a place ordained to be kept clean. The Qur'an's employment of the word *najas*, as opposed to *najis*, is often cited to corroborate the veracity of this conclusion, since the former signifies the capacity to transmit impurity as well as being able to be employed as a plural adjective.[107] By applying the jurisprudential notion of the priority (*awlawiyya*) of 'the concurrent implicative meaning' (*mafhūm al-muwāfaqa*) to the Qur'anic verse, the prohibition is extended to include disbelievers (*kāfirūn*) because they are deemed to be worse than polytheists ideologically due to their total opposition to God.[108] It should be noted that legists broadened the scope of the discourse on *najāsa* to include the *nāsibī* due to the *ḥadīth* literature stating instructions regarding all manner of interactions with them.[109]

Taqī al-Ṭabāṭabā'ī al-Qummī, in his commentary of al-Khū'ī's *Minhāj al-ṣāliḥīn*, refutes the assertion that the word *najas* in the Qur'anic verse signifies physical impurity, which is the crux of the aforementioned jurisprudential reasoning. He states that other Sharia-designated impure substances, such as blood, urine and dogs, were present in Mecca – hence, the claim that polytheists were banished due to their physical impurity does not hold true.[110] Furthermore, the conventions of having concubines and possessing slaves irrespective of religious persuasion was a prevalent practice within the Muslim community of the revelatory era,

106 Ibid. The bases for the Shī'ī legists' justifications are (a) reports implying the physical impurity of non-Muslims, and (b) Qur'anic verses deemed to be abrogating the (chronologically) later and more general Qur'anic verses presupposing their purity. According to them, the only 'purifier' of the physical impurity of non-Muslims is the profession of Islam. See Muḥammad Kāẓim al-Yazdī, *'Urwat al-Wuthqā* (Qum: Mu'assasat Ismā'īliyān, 1991), 1:108.

107 al-Ṭabrisī, *Majma' al-bayān fī tafsīr al-Qur'ān* (Beirut: Mu'assisa al-A'lamī li-l-Maṭbū'āt, 1995), 5:36–7.

108 For more information, see section *mafhūm al-muwāfaqa* in Muḥammad Ṣanqūr 'Alī, *al-Mu'jam al-uṣūlī* (Qum: Dār al-Mujtabā, 2001), 886–8.

109 For more information on the *nāsibī*, see al-Gharawī al-Tabrīzī, *al-Tanqīḥ fī sharḥ al-'urwat al-wuthqā taqrīran li-baḥth Āyatullāh al-Khū'ī* (Qum: Dār al-Hādī li-l-Maṭbū'āt, 1989), 3:76–7. For examples of general inclusion of the *nāṣibī* within the discourse of *najāsa*, see sections: (a) *Bāb taḥrīm nikāḥ al-nāṣiba al-mashhūra bi-dhālik*, and (b) *Bāb dhabā'iḥ man naṣaba al-'adāwa Āl Muḥammad*, in al-Ṭūsī, *al-Istibṣār*, 3:189–91 and 4:93–4. For a specific report utilising the word *najis* to refer to the *nāṣibī*, see footnote 42.

110 al-Ṭabāṭabā'ī, *Mabānī minhāj al-ṣāliḥīn*, 3:244–8.

that is, concubines and slaves did not have to belong to the Abrahamic faiths.[111] This indicates that today's understanding of the word *najis* as a notion signifying 'the physical impurity of the body caused by an erroneous belief system in spite of it being actually clean' would have been totally alien to these early Muslims. For them, the notion of *najis* would not have been applicable to the clean bodies of peoples subscribing to pagan belief-systems.[112] Similarly, the conduct of the *nāsibī* became a well-known phenomenon during the caliphate of the first Imām, yet neither the Imāms nor their companions treated the *nāṣibī* as impure entities, such as blood or urine.[113] On the contrary, it is reported that one of the wives of the fifth Imām vehemently despised the first Imām, and consequently he divorced her reluctantly; however, there is no indication that he considered her to be a physically impure substance.[114]

The root word *najas* (and *najāsa*) may be employed to describe the impure state or quality of two kinds of entities: sensorial (*najāsa ḥissiyya/ḥaqīqiyya*) and mental (*najāsa maʿnawiyya/ḥukmiyya*), that is, it can be used to refer to the state or quality of either sense-perceived objects or mental phenomena.[115] The category of mental impurity includes mental phenomena (such as thought, beliefs, dispositions, emotions and vices) that are morally and/or spiritually deficient.[116] Thus, the word *najas* in the Qur'anic verse is employed in the latter sense because it is used to describe the state of those who believe that God has associates/partners, which is a mental phenomenon, a belief.

111 See report no. 3 in al-Kulaynī, *Furūʿ al-Kāfī*, 5:361.

112 See footnotes 88 and 89 for reference to the sections in the four canonical works, wherein the reports are indicative of this. Also see al-ʿĀmilī, *Tafṣīl wasāʾil al-shīʿa*, 3:521–2. Finally, see the analytical discussion of purity status of the people of the Book in al-Ṭabāṭabāʾī, *Mabānī minhāj al-ṣāliḥīn*, 3:253–65.

113 For the historical beginnings of the phenomenon, see al-Gharwī, *al-Tanqīḥ fī sharḥ al-ʿurwa al-wuthqā*, 3: 77. Although aversion to the *nāṣibī* was expressed by the Imāms, they were not treated like urine or blood. See al-ʿĀmulī, *Tafṣīl wasāʾil al-shīʿa*, 3:518–20.

114 See report in B. Irwānī, *Durūs tamhīdiyya fī al-fiqh al-istidlālī ʿalā al-maḍhab al-Jaʿfarī* (Beirut: Dar al-Amīra, 2008), 2:386.

115 See Lane, Arabic-English Lexicon, 2: 2770.

116 Lane (the author of the Arabic-English Lexicon) notes that the transitive forms *naj-ja-sa* and *an-ja-sa* can be utilised to supply the meaning of 'making something "morally" unclean or dirty', that is, an entity is made to have a moral defect or blemish. The example he cites is the case of a man who fornicates with a woman, about which it may be said 'he has made her *najis*'. Furthermore, a person who performs a good deed after committing a morally reprehensible act is said to have cleansed himself of the blemish (*najāsa*) of that act. See ibid.

In conclusion, the employment of the word *najas* in the Qur'an vis-à-vis the polytheists merely signifies a state of deficiency in the moral and spiritual aspects of their minds or souls, just as its antonym, the word *ṭahāra*, is used to denote the inner or mental states of moral and spiritual purity. As such, the Qur'an's utility of the word *najas* does not signify the impurity of physical bodies. Therefore, reports expressing the 'impurity' of certain categories of human beings, such as the *majūs* or *nāsibī*, have to be understood as referring to the inner states of moral and spiritual impurity, and not the physical bodies. This is corroborated by Khū'ī in his *dars al-khārij* works. He states that reports instructing 'the washing of utensils used by the people of the book for the consumption of food and drink' must be understood in the context of their having been utilised – either actually or potentially – for the consumption of impure substances, such as pork.[117] Hence, the cause of such instructions cannot be considered to be the impure nature of the physical bodies of *ahl al-kitāb*, since the assertion that erroneous beliefs, or inner states of impurity, make the clean physical body impure is unjustified. Similarly, the prohibition of using public baths frequented by the Zoroastrians and Christians must be understood in the context of the uncleanliness of substances that remain as puddles in the baths after the bodies have been washed. This is because certain impure substances, such as urine and other substances, were not considered by them to be dirty, and hence in all likelihood they would have been upon their bodies prior to bathing.[118]

8. Survey of the Remaining Entities and Substances Designated as '*Najis*'

Reports addressing the purity status of substances considered by today's Sharia convention as 'impure substances' (*najāsāt*) are for the most part either: (a) conflicting and contradictory; or, (b) inconsistent with the attitudes and norms of the broader context of the revelatory era itself (*vis-à-vis* such impure

117 See al-Gharwī, *al-tanqīḥ fī sharḥ al-'urwa al-wuthqā*, 3:49-50. See also al-Ṭabāṭabā'ī, *Mabānī minhāj al-ṣāliḥīn*, 3:263–4. For examples of reports stating the rationale of the instruction to not partake of the food of *ahl al-kitāb*, see: (a) report no. 107 in Ibn Bābawayh al-Qummī, *Man lā yaḥḍaruhu al-faqīh*, 3:214.; (b) reports in al-Ṭūsī, *Tahdhīb al-aḥkām*, 9:81.

118 See reports in al-'Āmilī, *Tafṣīl wasā'il al-shī'a*, 1:218–20.

substances). In fact, such conflicting and contradictory reports are to be found regarding the issues of: (1) the status of devotional acts performed with impure substances on garments and/or the body; and (2) the prohibition of trading with impure substances.

The following is a brief survey of the Sharia-designated impure substances as delineated by the *fiqhī* discourse with a view to ascertaining: (a) those that actually warrant the Sharia designation of impurity; and (b) the nature, scope and implications of each Sharia-ordained impure substance. Thereafter, the section concludes with discussions on: (i) the status of devotional acts performed by individuals whose bodies or garments are sullied by the impure substances (*najāsāt*); and (ii) the status of trading with impure substances (*najāsāt*).

8.1 Wine

Several explicit (*ṣarīḥ*) reports state that wine is a pure substance whose presence on the body or garments does not affect the validity or discharging of the obligatory daily prayers (*ṣalawāt*).[119] In contrast to this, there are a lesser number of apparent (*ẓāhir*), or non-explicit (*gayr ṣarīḥ*) reports, declaring wine to be an impure substance that must be cleansed from contaminated garments prior to performing the obligatory prayers.[120] In light of the methodology of the existential framework (the relevant elements of which are mentioned above), the conclusion is that wine is not an impure substance as such, even though its consumption is impermissible and prohibited as per the instructions of the Qur'an.

8.2 Pig and Dog

The Qur'an is silent about the physical impurity of these animals; however, *ḥadīth* literature is emphatic in its instruction to cleanse utensils after dogs or pigs have consumed from them. At most, the reports convey the unhygienic quality of the bodily fluids of these animals vis-à-vis human beings.[121] More-

119 See reports 108–114 in al-Ṭūsī, *Tahdhīb al-aḥkām*, 1:291–3.

120 For the discussion on numbers and the analysis of two sets of contradictory reports, see al-Gharwī, *al-tanqīḥ fī sharḥ al-ʿurwa al-wuthqā*, 3:89–95. Also, for reports instructing the washing of garments, see 104–107 in al-Ṭūsī, *Tahdhīb al-aḥkām*, 1:290–1.

121 See reports 43–50 in ibid., 274–6 and al-Kulaynī, *Furūʿ al-Kāfī*, 3:68–9.

over, the inference of the Sharia-designated impurity (*najāsa*) of the physical bodies of dogs from reports such as, 'God has not created any creature as impure (*najis*) as the dog, but our enemy (*nāsibī*) is more impure (*anjas*) than a dog!', is flawed.[122] This is because it entails the logical fallacy of equivocation (*mushtarak lafẓī*): the word *najis* depicts the impurity of the physical body in relation to the dog, whereas it depicts an impure spiritual state in relation to the *nāsibī*. Consequently, the word *najis* in such reports has to be understood in light of the colloquial or everyday meaning of the sentence as a whole, and not its technical Sharia sense (since the latter entails a logical fallacy). Colloquially, the sentence has a hyperbolic signification emphasising the 'low' moral state or worth of the *nāsibī* in the view of the speaker, which in this case is the Imām. Hence, the word *najis* is being employed figuratively and not in its jurisprudential sense. Finally, there are reports implying that the purity of garments brushed by pigs are not compromised, and hence there is no implication on performing the daily prayers with the said garments.[123]

8.3 Dead Body

The majority of reports reiterate the Qur'anic prohibition of the consumption of dead animals.[124] As far as the impure status of dead bodies is concerned, the reports are emphatic regarding their detrimental and unhygienic nature.[125] They instruct that the point of contact with the dead body must either be washed in relation to indisposable objects such as a hand, or discarded, as in the case of foodstuff, or emptied of its contents *vis-à-vis* wells.[126] In spite of this, the prerequisite condition of 'ensuring garments or areas of the body sullied by contact with dead bodies are cleansed and pure' for the valid execution of the daily prayers, cannot be inferred satisfactorily from the reports. Perhaps the most significant issue in the *fiqhī* discourse pertaining to the dead body is in relation to wearing leather garments of animals not ritually slaughtered during the daily prayers. There are conflicting reports. Some reports permit praying the daily prayers with the leather garments of dead animals as long as: (a)

122 See footnote 42.

123 See reports in al-Ṭabāṭabā'ī, *Mabānī minhāj al-ṣāliḥīn*, 3:204-5 and 207–8.

124 See al-Ṭūsī, *al-Istibṣār* 4:65–67 and 94–95.

125 See reports in al-Ṭabāṭabā'ī, *Mabānī minhāj al-ṣāliḥīn*, 3:151–60.

126 Ibid.

they cover the non-mandatory parts of the body not required to be covered by *ḥalāl* (permissible) garments (such as socks); or (b) they are accessories (such as belts).[127] Therefore, since the wearing of leather garments of dead animals is permissible, its corollary of trading with such items of clothing ought to be permitted too.

8.4 Blood and Urine

The Qur'an prohibits the consumption of blood and declares it as 'filth' (*rijs*), but it is silent regarding urine.[128] The reports stress the imperative of ensuring the body and garments are cleansed of blood and urine prior to engaging in the daily prayers.[129] Exceptions to this ruling are made in the verdicts of the legists, such as the non-problematic nature of drops of urine splashed on the body and garments during the use of the lavatory, and the admissibility of a minimal quantity of blood on garments.[130] Such exceptions imply that the nature of the impurity of these substances pertain to hygiene, the lack of which is inconducive to the inner state of spiritual cleanliness in general. In fact, there is a report stating that, in the absence of water, one's saliva may be employed to remove impurities from the genitalia.[131] Therefore, the inflexibility associated with the prerequisite condition, of ensuring every speck of these substances are cleansed from the body and garments for the validity of the daily prayers and entering mosques, is unwarranted.

8.5 Semen

Reports state that semen is an impure substance; hence, it is necessary for the body and garments to be cleansed of it prior to performing the daily prayers. However, some reports sourced in both the Shī'ī and Sunnī compilations of *aḥādīth* permit the performance of the daily prayers in garments with dry semen.[132]

---

127 See the reports and discussion in al-Ṭabāṭabā'ī, *Mabānī minhāj al-ṣāliḥīn*, 3:421–3.

128 See Qur'an 6:145.

129 See al-Kulaynī, *Furū' al-Kāfī*, 3:62–4 and 66–68.

130 See al-Yazdī, *'Urwat al-Wuthqā*, 1:32. For admissibility of minimal quantity of blood on garments during prayers, see al-'Āmulī, *Tafṣīl wasā'il al-shī'a*, 3:429–32.

131 See report no. 4 in al-Kulaynī, *Furū' al-Kāfī*, 3:25.

132 See report no. 7 in al-'Āmilī, *Tafṣīl wasā'il al-shī'a*, 3:446.

8.6 The Status of Devotional Acts

In light of the above, the applicability of the designation of 'impurity' to a clean human body is not established by Sharia texts. A clean human body irrespective of its ideological persuasion is not the subject-matter of the designation of 'impurity', hence it is to be considered as materially and substantially pure, which stands to reason. Similarly, explicit reports (*aḥādīth ṣarīḥa*) state that wine is not a *najis* substance in itself. As far as the rest of the *najāsāt* are concerned, the Qur'an – which constitutes the 'heavier weight of the two weights' – is silent regarding their respective purity statuses. The Qur'anic instruction is to ensure garments, and thus the body by priority, are kept clean of filth. However, the prerequisite of the necessity of ensuring the body and garments are absolutely free of the impure substances for the daily prayers to be valid cannot be ascertained from the Qur'an. Moreover, *ḥadīth* literature either conflicts or is inconclusive vis-à-vis this prerequisite advocating such a strict sense of cleanliness.

Therefore, in light of the survey and the aforementioned elements of the methodology of the existential framework, the conclusion is that Sharia-designated impure substances (*najāsāt*) are detrimental at a physical level, hence their ingestion is prohibited, and it is obligatory to cleanse contaminated body parts and garments. Furthermore, since impure substances are inconducive to a person's inner spiritual state, the body and garments must be clean before executing the daily prayers by priority. Therefore, in light of the spirit of Qur'an and *ḥadīth* literature, bodies and garments must be kept clean of the impure substances both in the general context of everydayness and during prayers, but within reason. That being said, their mere presence on the body and garments cannot be said to impede the validity of prayers in the strictest sense. This is because the essence of devotional behaviours (*rūḥ al-ʿibādāt*) is 'the intentionality of devotion' (*al-rūḥ al-khāṣṣa li-l-ʿibāda*), which is not contingent upon the cleanliness or impurity of the body or garments per se.[133]

133 For information on the expression *al-rūḥ al-khāṣṣ li-l-ḥukm*, see footnote 5.

8.7 The Status of Trading with Impure Substances

The following Prophetic report epitomises the evidences cited by legists for the prohibition of trading with Sharia-designated impure substances (*najāsāt*): 'When God prohibits something, He also prohibits its sale-price.'[134] Based on this and other similar reports, legists assert that impure substances cannot have any benefit in relation to human beings; rather, they are detrimental, and hence there cannot be any value in trading with them in the mind of God.[135] Consequently, such trade would entail 'the consumption of wealth in a wrongful manner'.[136] Accordingly, the prohibition of trading with such substances is deemed to be both normative (*taklīfī*) and status-based (*waḍʿī*) in the *fiqhī* discourse, which means such trading is not only invalid, but sinful. Legists do admit some exceptions to this general rule on the basis of reports exempting the ownership of guard and hunting dogs, and contaminated oil and fat utilised for lighting purposes.[137]

The Qur'an makes no allusion to the prohibition of the ownership and transaction of the Sharia-designated impure substances. As regards *ḥadīth* literature, there are reports both approving and prohibiting such trade, hence it is not possible to prohibit all forms of such trade conclusively.[138] In light of the existential properties of 'no finality' and 'flux in factuality', the aforementioned Prophetic report signifies a qualified prohibition of trading with the impure substances, and not an absolute one: the prohibition is restricted to 'the buying and selling of an impure substance with a view to utilising it in the manner for which it was prohibited', and not otherwise.[139] This signification is corroborated by other similar reports, such as the famous report of the sixth

134 See footnote 40.

135 For instance, see Murtaḍā Anṣārī, *Kitāb al-Makāsib* (Qum: Intishārāt Ismāʿīliyān, 1995), 1:10.

136 Reference to recurring phrase in numerous Qur'anic verses, such 2:188, 4:29 and 9:34.

137 For reports stating the permissibility of owning guard and hunting dogs, and contaminated oil and fat, see Anṣārī, *Kitāb al-makāsib*, 1:19–20 and 23.

138 For instance, there reports prohibiting and permitting the trade of faeces. See Anṣārī, *Kitāb al-makāsib*, 1:11.

139 The existential property of 'no finality' is a derivative of the existential property of growth. In the domain of Sharia regulations, it signifies the impossibility of asserting absoluteness, or the absolute unrestrictedness and applicability, to any regulative proposition or formulation. In other words, the nature of existence dictates that there can never be 'finality' to any particular regulative formulation in the mind of God.

Imām in *Tuḥaf al-ʿuqūl* delineating the permissible and impermissible forms of trade.[140] Furthermore, it seems that the conventional utility of the impure substances prior to their being prohibited was often limited to the behaviour that the Sharia prohibited, that is, they were not conventionally used in other domains productively. This is evinced by the lack of reports expressing exceptions, such as those mentioned above regarding the permissibility of the ownership and transaction of: (a) contaminated oil for lighting purposes; and (b) dogs for guarding farms.

Qualifying the aforesaid Prophetic report is also warranted in light of the Prophet permitting *ahl al-kitāb*: (i) to own, rear, sell and consume pigs, and (ii) to brew, sell and consume alcoholic beverages amongst themselves.[141] At most, this implies that only Muslims *qua* Muslims cannot own or sell such things; that is, these prohibitions have force only within Muslim existential contexts, and hence such prohibitions do not apply to non-Muslims and non-Muslim existential contexts. Finally, *ḥadīth* literature also states the prohibition of trading with items contributing to societal corruption.[142] This general precept prohibits the trade of the tools of gambling (such as packs of cards and chess boards and pieces) and other intoxicants not mentioned in *ḥadīth* literature. Obviously, the cause for the prohibition of trading with such entities is not the notion of impurity (*najis*), rather it is societal corruption.[143]

In summary, the prohibition of trading with impure substances (*najāsāt*) was due to one or both of the following reasons: either (1) the non-existence of a befitting, productive and beneficial utility besides the one prohibited; or (2) the risk posed to the Muslim individual and collectivity of reverting back to the prohibited utility should trading with the prohibited substance for its other utilities be permitted. In light of this, trading with impure substances will be permissible, if: (1) befitting, productive and beneficial utilities of the impure substances are conceived of; and (2) if it is assessed that trading with the impure substances in the capacity of their beneficial utilities does not pose the risk of (a) societal corruption, (b) reversion back to the prohibited behaviours vis-à-vis Muslims and their existential contexts, and (c) moral and spiritual detriment to the Muslim individual and collectivity.

---

140 See report in Anṣārī, *Kitāb al-makāsib*, 1:5.

141 This is a historical fact verified presuppositionally by *ḥadīth* literature.

142 This is mentioned in *Tuḥaf al-ʿuqūl*. See footnote 142 and also Anṣārī, *Kitāb al-makāsib*, 1:42.

143 Ibid.

Conclusion

After the major occultation of the twelfth Imām, the purity status of the bodies of non-Muslims gradually changed from purity to impurity in Shī'ī Imāmī jurisprudence. Prior to the fifth century, there was no unanimity among Shī'ī scholars regarding the intrinsic impurity of the body of non-Muslims. It was only from the fifth century onwards that a consensus was reached regarding this impurity, contravening Qur'anic verses presupposing the physical purity of non-Muslims. The motivation for this seems to have been the predominant attitude of the time, namely, the mentality of superiority over other Muslims. In other words, this change in the purity status of non-Muslims seems to have been the effect of the zeitgeist of Shī'ī scholars of that time, which was to adopt contrary regulative norms to those of other Muslims, and then to highlight the superiority of their norms over those of the latter. In light of this, and upon analysis of the religious texts, this paper posits the purity of the bodies and bodily fluids of all non-Muslims.

This paper also posits the purity of wine and other alcoholic substances based on explicit reports (*aḥādīth ṣarīha*) within *ḥadīth* literature presupposing the purity of wine in itself.

The Qur'an is silent regarding the purity status of the rest of the impure substances (*najāsāt*). It instructs that garments, and thus the body by priority, are to be kept clean of filth in the context of everydayness. The prerequisite of ensuring the body and garments are free of impure substances for the daily prayers to be valid, although implied in the Qur'anic exhortation of cleanliness, has explicit expression in *ḥadīth* literature. Therefore, it is obligatory to cleanse contaminated body parts and garments in the context of everydayness and as a prerequisite to the daily prayers.

This paper concludes that Sharia-designated impure substances are detrimental at a physical level fundamentally (hence their ingestion is prohibited), but also have consequences for the moral and spiritual aspects of the mind or soul.

Finally, the prohibition of trading with impure substances is not absolute. Trading with them is possible if their other utilities (besides their prohibited ones) are beneficial to society, and as long as there is no risk of Muslims reverting back to their prohibited utilities.

www.ingramcontent.com/pod-product-compliance
Lightning Source LLC
Chambersburg PA
CBHW071526080526
44588CB00011B/1568
9781915550002